Buddhism
The Religion of No-Religion

ALAN WATTS
at a seminar aboard the SS *Vallejo,* 1966

Alan Watts

Buddhism
The Religion of No-Religion

Introduction by Mark Watts

TUTTLE Publishing

Tokyo | Rutland, Vermont | Singapore

Dedicated to the living teachings
of Shunryu Suzuki, Roshi

Contents

Introduction

The widespread influence of Buddhism is due in part to the skill with which a way of liberation, first taught in ancient India, was refined by its teachers and became accessible to people of diverse cultures. For, as Alan Watts commented during a seminar aboard his ferryboat home in Sausalito, California, in the late sixties:

The Hindus, the Buddhists, and many other ancient peoples do not, as we do, make a division between religion and everything else. Religion is not a department of life; it is something that enters into the whole of it. But when a religion and a culture are inseparable, it is very difficult to export a religion, because it comes into conflict with the established traditions, manners, and customs of other people.

So the question arises, what are the essentials of Hinduism that could be exported? And when you answer that question, you will find Buddhism. As I explained, the essence of Hinduism, the real deep root, is not a kind of doctrine or even a special kind of discipline, although of course disciplines are involved. The center of Hinduism is an experience of liberation called *moksha*, in which, through the dissipation of the illusion that each man and woman is a separate thing in a world consisting of nothing but a collection of separate things, you discover that you are, in a way, on one level an illusion, but on another level you are what they call the self, the one self, which is all that there is.

Alan Watts's interest in Eastern thought can be followed back to his childhood, where he was surrounded by Oriental art. His mother was a teacher for the children of missionaries who traveled abroad, and often on their return from China the missionaries would give her gifts of embroideries and landscape paintings in the style of the great classical Asian artists. Years later, while on tour in Japan with a small group of students, Watts recounted the origins of his interest in the arts and philosophies of the Far East:

I had an absolute fascination for Chinese and Japanese secular painting—the landscapes, the treatment of flowers and grasses and bamboo. There was something about that treatment that struck me as astonishing, even though the subject matter was extremely ordinary. Even as a child I had to find out what that strange element in those bamboo and grasses was. I was, of course, being taught by those painters to see grass, but there was something else in their paintings I could never put my finger on. That "something else" was the thing I will call the religion of no-religion. It is the supreme attainment of a buddha: it cannot be detected; it leaves no trace.

As a young man growing up in Kent, England, Alan Watts's curiosity about the philosophies of Asia led him to explore the bookstores around Cambridge and eventually to the Buddhist Lodge in London. He attended lodge meetings with Christmas Humphreys and soon met the Zen Buddhist scholar D. T. Suzuki. Watts's formative articles on Buddhism are found in his collected early writings, and they reflect an understanding of Buddhist thought quite advanced for his time. His two subsequent books on Zen Buddhism enjoyed widespread popularity, and by the early sixties Alan Watts was living in California, writing extensively on Eastern thought, and conducting regular speaking tours across the country and in Europe. During this period Alan Watts traveled to Japan twice— once in 1963 and again in 1965. It was on the second Japan tour that he recorded himself in a series of talks that have come to be known as the Japan Seminars. Today these sessions offer one of the most readily comprehensible introductions to Buddhism available in the English language. Watts presents the essential tenets of Buddhism in a concise form, rich with illustrative stories and infused with the spirit in which this great tradition has evolved. The current volume is composed of four sessions from the Japan Seminars—*The Journey from India, The Middle Way, Religion of No-Religion*, and *Buddhism* As *Dialogue*—and two sessions on Tibetan Buddhism recorded four years later in 1969 aboard his ferryboat in Sausalito, California—*Wisdom of the Mountains* and *Transcending Duality*. These selections provide an intimate overview of the development of Buddhist thought and offer an introduction to one of the world's most fascinating ways of liberation.

—Mark Watts
August 1995

Buddhism
The Religion of No-Religion

is the Hindu view of the world as a drama, looked at as a play. Third is the organic Chinese view, looking on the world as an organism, a body. But the Hindu view sees it as a drama, or simply that there is what there is, and always was, and always will be, which is called the self; in Sanskrit, *atman*. Atman is also called brahman, from the root *bri*: to grow, to expand, to swell, related to our word *breath*. Brahman, the self in the Hindu worldview, plays hide-and-seek with itself forever and ever. How far out, how lost can you get? According to the Hindu idea, each one of us is the godhead, getting lost on purpose for the fun of it. And how terrible it gets at times! But won't it be nice when we wake up? That's the basic idea, and I've found that any child can understand it. It has great simplicity and elegance.

This cosmology or conception of the universe has many features, including the *kalpas*, or vast periods of time through which the universe passes. Another aspect is the six worlds, or paths of life. This idea of six worlds is very important in Buddhism, although it comes from Hinduism, and is represented in what is called the *phava chakra*. *Phava* means "becoming"; *chakra* means "wheel." The wheel of becoming, or wheel of birth and death, has six divisions. The people on top are called *devas*. The people on the bottom are called *naraka*. Devas are angels, the people who are the supreme worldly successes. The naraka are tormented in hell and they are the supreme worldly failures. These are the poles: the happiest people and the saddest people. In between comes the world of the *pretas*, or hungry ghosts, next to the naraka in hell. The pretas are the frustrated spirits who have tiny mouths and enormous bellies—huge appetites but very limited means of satisfying them. Next up from the pretas are the human beings. They are supposed to hold a middle position in the six worlds. Then you go up from the human beings to the devas and then you start coming down again. The next world is called the *asura*, in which are the wrathful spirits, personifications of scorn and of all the anger and violence of nature. Next down are the animals, coming between the asura and the hells.

These needn't be taken literally; they are different modalities of the human mind. We are in the naraka world when we are frustrated and in torment. When we are merely chronically frustrated we are in the preta world. When we are in a state of equanimity or even-mindedness, we are in the human world. When we are deliriously happy we are in the deva world. When we are furious we are in the asura world. And when we are dumb we are in the animal world. These are all modalities, and it is terribly important to understand that in Buddhism, the better you get, the more you go up to the deva world, the worse you get, the more you go down to the naraka world. Everything that goes up has to come down; you can't improve yourself indefinitely. If you improve yourself beyond a certain limit you simply start to get worse, like when you make a knife too sharp and it begins to wear away. Buddhahood, liberation, or enlightenment is not on any place on the wheel, unless it might be the center. By ascending, by becoming better, you tie yourself to the wheel by golden chains. By retrogressing and becoming worse, you tie yourself to the wheel with iron chains. But the Buddha is the one who gets rid of the chains altogether.

This explains why Buddhism, unlike Judaism and Christianity, is not frantically concerned with being good; it is concerned with being wise. It is concerned with being compassionate, which is a little different from being good, with having tremendous sympathy and understanding and respect for all the ignorant people who don't know that they're it but who are playing the very far-out game of being "you and I." This is why every Hindu greets his brother not by shaking hands but by putting his hands together and bowing. And this is basically why the Japanese bow to each other, and why the Buddhist rituals are full of the bowing gesture, because you are honoring the self playing the roles of all the people around you. All the more honor is due when the self has forgotten what it is doing and is therefore in a very far-out situation. That is the basic Hindu view of the world, and the cosmology that goes along with Buddhism.

According to taste, temperament, tradition, popular belief, and so on, there is this additional idea that when the lord, or self, pretends that it is each of us, it first of all pretends that it is an individual soul called the *jivat-man*. The jivatman reincarnates through a whole series of bodies, life after life after life. According to what is called karma, literally meaning "doing" or "the law of doing," acts occur in a series and are linked with each other in an unbreakable chain. Everybody's karma is the life course that he will work out through perhaps innumerable lifetimes. I'm not going into that, because a lot of Buddhists do not believe it.

For example, Zen people are quite divided on this, and say they don't believe literally in reincarnation—that after your funeral you suddenly become somebody different, living somewhere else. They say reincarnation means that if you, sitting here now, are really convinced that you are the same person who walked in the door half an hour ago, you are being reincarnated. If you are liberated, you will understand that you are not. The past does not exist; the future does not exist. There is only the present. That is the only real you that there is. Zen master Dogen put it this way, "Spring does not become summer. First there is spring and then there is summer. Each season stays in its own place." In the same way, the you of yesterday does not become the you of today. T. S. Eliot has the same idea in his poem *Four Quartets*, where he says that when you settle down in the train to read your newspaper, you are not the same person who, a little while before, left the platform. If you think you are, you are linking up your moments in a chain. This is what binds you to the wheel of birth and death, unlike when you know that every moment where you are is the only moment. So a Zen master will say to somebody, "Get up and walk across the room." And when they come back he asks, "Where are your footprints?" They've gone.

Where are you? Who are you? When we are asked who we are, we usually give a kind of recitation of a history. "I'm So-and-so. I was given this name by my parents. I've been to such-and-such a college. I've done these things in my profession." And we produce a little biography. The

Buddhist says, "Forget it; that's not you. That is some story that's all past. I want to see the real you, the you you are now." Nobody knows who that is, because we do not know ourselves except through listening to our echoes and consulting our memories. But then the real you leads us back to this question, Who is the real you? We shall see how they play with this in Zen koans to get you to come out of your shell and find out who you really are.

In India this worldview is tied up with a whole culture involving every circumstance of everyday life, but Hinduism is not a religion in the same sense that Episcopalianism or even Roman Catholicism are. Hinduism is not a religion, it is a culture. In this respect it's more like Judaism than Christianity, because a person is still recognizable as a Jew even though they don't go to synagogue. Jewish people, coming from a line of Jewish parents and ancestors who have been practicing Jews, still continue certain cultural ways of doing things, certain mannerisms and attitudes, so they are cultural Jews instead of religious Jews. Hinduism is the same sort of thing; it is a religious culture. Being a Hindu really involves living in India. Because of the differences of climate, of arts, crafts, and technology, you cannot be a Hindu in the full sense in Japan or in the United States.

Buddhism is Hinduism stripped for export. The Buddha was a reformer in the highest sense: someone who wants to go to the original form, or to re-form it for the needs of a certain time. The word *buddha* is a title, not a proper name, in the same way as *Christ* means "the anointed" and is not the surname of Jesus. "Buddha" is not the surname of Gautama, but means "the one who is awakened" (from the root in Sanskrit *budh*, to know); Buddha is the man who woke up, who discovered who he really was.

The crucial issue wherein Buddhism differs from Hinduism is that it doesn't say who you are; it has no idea, no concept. I emphasize the words *idea* and *concept*. It has no idea and no concept of God because Buddhism is not interested in concepts, it is interested in direct experience only. From the Buddhist standpoint all concepts are wrong, in the same way that nothing is really what you say it is. Is this a stool? When I turn it over—now it's a wastebasket. When I beat on it, it's a drum. So this thing is what it does. Anything you can use it for is what it is. If you have a rigid idea that it is a stool and you can only sit on it, you're kind of stuck. But if you see all these other things as well, then you suddenly see that anything can be everything. In the same way, Buddhism does not say that what you really are is something definable, because if you believe that, you are stuck with an idea and cling to it for spiritual security.

A lot of people say they want a religion as something to hold on to. A Buddhist would say to cut that out. As long as you hold on to something, you do not have religion. You are only really there when you let go of everything and do not depend on any fixed idea or belief for your sanity or happiness. You might think Buddhism is very destructive, because it breaks down or does not believe in God. It does not believe in an immortal soul or seek any solace in any idea of life after death. It absolutely faces the fact of the transiency of life. There is nothing you can hold on to, so let go. There is no one to hold on to anything, anyway. Buddhism is the discipline of doing that. But if you do that, you see, you discover something much better than any belief, because you have got the real thing, only you cannot say what it is.

They say in Zen that if you are enlightened you are like a dumb man who has had a wonderful dream. When you have had a wonderful dream you want to tell everybody what it is, but you cannot if you are dumb, if you cannot speak. The real thing in Buddhism, which they call nirvana, is sort of equivalent to moksha, or liberation. Nirvana means "to blow out"—the sigh of relief—because if you hold your breath, you lose it. If you hold on to yourself, you hold on to life or the breath or spirit; you hold on to God. Then it is all dead; it becomes just a rock, just an idol. But let go, breathe out, and you get your breath back. That's nirvana.

The Buddhists' doctrine is the highest negativism. They characterize the ultimate reality as *sunyata*, which means emptiness; in Japanese this is ku, the character used for the sky or the air. When you get an airmail envelope to write home, the second character is *ku*, air, which means emptiness. They use this character to translate *sunyata*, emptiness; the fundamental nature of reality, the sky. But the sky is not negative emptiness; it contains all of us. It is full of everything that is happening, but you cannot put a nail in the sky and pin it down. In the same way, Buddhism is saying that you do not need any gizmos to be in the know. You do not need a religion. You do not need any Buddha statues, temples, Buddhist rosaries, and all that jazz. But when you get to the point that you know you do not need any of those things, you do not need a religion at all; then it is fun to have one. Then you can be trusted to use rosaries, ring bells, hit drums and clappers, and chant sutras. But those things will not help you a bit. They will just tie you up in knots if you use them as methods of catching hold of something. So every teacher of Buddhism is a debunker, not to be a smart aleck and show how clever he is, but out of compassion. Just as when a surgeon chops off a bad growth or a dentist pulls out a rotten tooth, so the Buddhist teacher is getting rid of your crazy ideas for you, which you use to cling to life and make it dead.

There are two kinds of Buddhism, the first called Mahayana; *maha* is Sanskrit for "great"; *yana* means a vehicle or conveyance. The other is Hinayana, meaning the little vehicle; *hina* in Sanskrit means "little." That term was invented by the Mahayanists for the other people, who don't like it. They call themselves Theravada, which means: *vada*, the way; *thera*, of the elders. Theravada Buddhism you find now in Ceylon, Burma, Thailand, Cambodia, and generally South Asia. Mahayana you find in Nepal and northern India, where it originated, and in Tibet, China, Mongolia, Japan, and, to some extent, Indonesia. All the sects of Japanese Buddhism are Mahayana.

What is the great difference between these two schools? The Theravada is very strict. It is a way for monks, essentially, rather than laymen. There are many ways of living Buddhism. The Theravada Buddhists are trying to live without desires: to have no need for wives or girlfriends, husbands or boyfriends; not to kill anything at all; living the strictest vegetarian way; and even straining their water so that they do not eat any little insects with it. Also in this very strict way, they meditate all the time and eventually attain nirvana, which involves total disappearance from the manifested world.

Mahayana feels that that is a dualistic point of view. You do not need to get away from this world to experience nirvana, because nirvana is what there is. It is here; it is now. The ideal person of Mahayana is called a bodhisattva. This originally meant somebody on the way to becoming a buddha, but in Mahayana it means somebody who has become a buddha but has gone back into the world, in the spirit of compassion, in order to help all other beings to become awakened. And that is an endless task, like filling a well with snow. Putting snow into a well, it never fills up. At the Zen monastery, after they have said their homage to the Buddha, the dharma, which is the Buddha's doctrine or method, and the *sangha*, the order of followers of the Buddha, then they take four vows, and one of them is "However innumerable sentient beings are, I vow to liberate them all." So there is no end to that; there never comes a time when all sentient beings are liberated. But from the standpoint of one who is a buddha, everybody is liberated. In other words, a buddha would not say, "Look everybody, I'm a buddha. I'm more experienced than you, and I know more than you, and you owe me respect on that account." On the other hand, a buddha would see you all as being exactly right; just where you are, all of you are buddhas. Even for those of you who do not know it, it is right for you not to know it at this moment.

It is absolutely fundamental to an understanding of Buddhism to recognize that its whole method of teaching is dialectical. It consists of a dialogue between a teacher and a student. The method of this dialogue is called *upaya*, or "skillful means" used by the teacher to bring about the enlightenment of the student. Upaya implies expert pedagogy in teaching, but "deceit," when used in a political context. Since Buddhism is a dialogue, what you ordinarily understand as the teachings of Buddhism are not the teachings of Buddhism, they are simply the opening gambit or process of this dialogue. The point is that Buddhism is not a teaching. Its essence consists in a certain kind of experience, a transformation of consciousness, which is called awakening or enlightenment, that involves our seeing through or transcending the hoax of being a separate ego. A Buddhist does not have the same tendency that a Christian has to want to find out what his faith is by going back to the most original sources. There has always been a tendency in Christianity to ask, "What did Jesus really teach? What is the pure New Testament, uncorrupted by theologians and by scribes who inserted things into the mouth of the master?"

It does not occur to Buddhists to have this attitude because of this dialectic pattern. When you have an acorn, if it is a lively acorn it grows into an oak. That is the way it should be, it should develop into something. And just so Buddhism, as it has developed since the days of the Buddha, has gone a long way. It has become sometimes more complex, sometimes more simple, but it has changed radically because the seed that the Buddha planted was alive. For example, when we ask what the Buddhist scriptures are we might get two answers. In the Southern (Theravada) school there is a set of scriptures written in the Pali language, that are divided into three sections, called the Tripitaka, which means "three baskets," because the palm-leaf manuscripts on which these sutras were eventually written down were carried around in baskets, and three baskets of these palm-leaf manuscript volumes composed the Buddhist scriptures.

However, in the evolution of these scriptures, the Buddha himself wrote nothing, nor did his immediate disciples. It is very important to remember that all Indian scriptures were, for many centuries, handed down orally. We have no clear guide as to their dates, because in handing down an oral tradition you are not always likely to preserve historical landmarks. Suppose we are talking about a certain king, and the name of this king will mark a historical point. In an oral tradition the name of the king is likely to be changed every time the story is told, to correspond to the king then reigning. Things that do change, that have a historical rhythm like a succession of kings, will be changed in handing down the oral tradition. But things that do not change, such as the essential principle of the doctrine, will not be altered at all. So remember that the Buddhist scriptures were handed down orally for some hundreds of years before they were ever committed to writing, and that accounts for their monotonous form.

Everything is numbered; there are four noble truths,

eight steps of the eightfold path, ten fetters, five *skandhas*, four *brahma-viharas* or meditation states, and so on. Everything is put in numerical lists so as to be memorized easily. Formulas are constantly repeated, and this is supposed to aid the memory. It is obvious that those scriptures of the Pali canon, when you really sit down and read them, have a certain monotony because of mnemonic aids, but also that, in the course of the time before they were written down, many monks spent wet afternoons adding to them and adding things in such a style that no inspired person would ever have said them. They have made commentaries on commentaries, and lots of them had no sense of humor. I always loved the passage where the Buddha is giving instructions on the art of meditation and he is describing a number of things on which one could concentrate. A commentator is making little notes on this and has made his list of things on which you could concentrate, like a square drawn on the ground or the tip of your nose or a leaf or a stone, and then it says, "or on anything." The commentator adds the footnote, "but not any wicked thing." That's professional clergy for you, the world over.

This sort of thing has obviously happened. But this accumulation, with attribution of one's own writings to the Buddha, is not done in a dishonest way. It would be dishonest today with our standards of literary historicity and correctness. It would be very wrong of me to forge a document and pretend that it was written by some very venerable person, say by D. T. Suzuki or by Goethe. But centuries ago, both in the West and in the East, it was considered quite immoral to publish any book of wisdom under your own name, because you, personally, were not entitled to the possession of this knowledge. That is why you always put on any book of wisdom the name of the real author, that is the person who inspired you. In this way, it is perfectly certain that Solomon never wrote the Book of The Wisdom of Solomon. But it was attributed to Solomon because Solomon was an archetype of the wise man. In the same way, over the centuries, when various Buddhist monks and scholars wrote all kinds of sutras, or scriptures, and ascribed them to the Buddha, they were being properly modest. They were saying that these doctrines are not my doctrines, they are the doctrines that proceed from the Buddha in me, and therefore they should be ascribed to Buddha. And so over and above the Pali canon, there is an enormous corpus of scriptures written originally in Sanskrit and subsequently translated into Chinese and Tibetan. We have very inadequate manuscripts of the original Sanskrit, but we have very complete Chinese and Tibetan translations.

It is primarily from Chinese and Tibetan sources that we have the Mahayana canon of scriptures, over and above the Theravada canon written in the Pali language. Pali is a softened form of Sanskrit. Whereas in Sanskrit one says "nirvana," in Pali one says "nibbana." Sanskrit says "karma"; Pali says "kamma." Sanskrit says "dharma"; Pali says "dhamma." It is a very similar language, but it is softer in its speech and articulation. It is a general feeling among scholars of the West today that the Pali scriptures are closer to the authentic teachings of the Buddha than the Sanskrit ones. With our Christian background and approach to scriptures, the West has built up a very strong prejudice in favor of the authenticity of the Theravada tradition as against the Mahayana tradition.

The Mahayanists have a hierarchy of scriptures, the first for very simpleminded people. Next are about four grades, going progressively to the scriptures for the most insightful people. They say that the Buddha preached these to his intimate disciples first. Then slowly, as he reached out from the most intimate group to others, he came down to what is now the Pali canon, as the scriptures for the biggest dunderheads, but the ones he preached first were not revealed until long, long after his death. So the Mahayanists have no difficulty in making a consistent story about the fact that the scriptures in Sanskrit represent a level of historical evolution of Buddhist ideas that, from our point of view, could not possibly have been attained in the Buddha's lifetime. But they say that the latest revealed was actually the first taught to the inmost disciples.

We have to make allowances for these differences in points of view, and not entirely project Western standards of historical and documentary criticism onto Buddhist scriptures, because it is in the essence of Buddhism to be a developing process in dialogue. The initial steps of the dialogue are in the presumed earliest records of Buddhism. In the Four Noble Truths, it says that the problem that Buddhism faces is suffering. This word *duhkha*, which we translate as "suffering," is the opposite of *suhkha*. Suhkha means what is sweet and delightful. Duhkha means the opposite, the bitter and frustrating. Mahayanists explain that the Buddha always taught by a dialectical method.

That is, when people were trying to make the goal of life the pursuit of suhkha, or the pursuit of happiness, he counteracted this wrong view by teaching that life is essentially miserable. When people thought that there was a permanent and eternal self in each one of us, and clung to that self, in order to counteract this one-sided view, the Buddha taught the other extreme doctrine, that there is no fixed self in us, no ego. But a Mahayanist would always say that the truth is the Middle Way, neither suhkha nor duhkha, neither atman nor *anatman*, self nor nonself. This is the whole point.

Once R. H. Blyth was asked by some students, "Do you believe in God?" He answered, "If you do, I don't. If you don't, I do." In much the same way, all Buddhist pedagogy is specifically addressed not to people in general, but to the individual who brings a problem. Wherever he seems to be overemphasizing things in one way, the teacher overemphasizes in the opposite way so as to arrive at the middle way. So this emphasis on life as suffering is simply saying that the problem we are dealing with is that we hurt. We human beings feel pretty unfairly treated because we are born into a world arranged so that the price we pay for enjoying it, for having sensitive bodies, is that these bodies are capable of the most excruciating agonies. Isn't that a nasty trick to play on us? What are we going to do about it? This is the problem.

When the Buddha says, "The cause of suffering is desire," the word translated as desire might better be something like "craving," "clinging," or "grasping." He is saying, "I'm suggesting that you suffer because you desire." Then suppose you try not to desire, and see if by not desiring you can cease from suffering. You could put the same thing in another way by saying to a person, "It's all in your mind. There is nothing either good or ill, but thinking makes it so." Therefore, if you can control your mind you have nothing else that you need control. You do not need to control the rain if you can control your mind. If you get wet it is only your mind that makes you think it's uncomfortable to be wet. A person who has good mental discipline can be perfectly happy wandering around in the rain. You do not need a fire if you have good mind control. But if you have ordinary, bad mind control, when it is cold you start shivering because you are putting up a resistance to the cold; you are fighting it. But don't fight it, relax to the cold, as a matter of mental attitude, and then you will be fine. Always control your mind. This is another way of approaching it.

As soon as the student begins to experiment with these things, he finds out that it is not so easy as it sounds. Not only is it very difficult not to desire, or to control your mind, but there is something phony about the whole business. This is exactly what you are intended to discover—that when you try to eliminate desire in order to escape from suffering, you desire to escape from suffering. You are desiring not to desire. I am not merely playing with logic but saying that a person who is escaping from reality will always feel the terror of it. It will be like the hound of heaven that pursues him. In a way he is escaping even when he tries not to escape. This is the point that this method of teaching was supposed to educate about and draw out from you. The first step is not to explain all this to you but to make the experiment not to desire, or the experiment to control your mind thoroughly. To understand this, you must go through some equivalent of that so as to come to the point where you see you are involved in a vicious circle. In trying to control your mind, the motivation is still clinging and grasping, still self-protection, lack of trust and love. When this is understood, the student returns to the teacher and says, "This is my difficulty, I cannot eliminate desire because my effort to do so is itself desire. I cannot eliminate selfishness because my reasons for wanting to be unselfish are selfish."

As one of the Chinese Buddhist classics puts it, "When the wrong man uses the right means, the right means work in the wrong way." Right means are all the traditional disciplines you use. You practice *zazen* and make yourself into a buddha. But if you are not a buddha in the first place, you cannot become one, because you will be the wrong man. You are using the right means, but because you are using them for a selfish or fearful intent, you are afraid of suffering; you do not like it and you want to escape. These motivations frustrate the right means. One is meant to find that out.

In time, as this was thoroughly explored by the Buddha's disciples, there developed a very evolved form of this whole dialectic technique, which was called *Madhyamika*, meaning the middle way. It was a form of Buddhist practice and instruction developed by Nagarjuna, who lived in approximately 200 A.D. Nagarjuna's method is simply an extension to logical conclusions of the method of dialogue that already existed, except that Nagarjuna took it to an extreme. His method is simply to undermine and cast doubts on any proposition to which his student clings, to destroy all intellectual formulations and conceptions, whatsoever, about the nature of reality or the nature of the self.

You might think this was simply a parlor game, a little intellectual exercise. But if you engaged in it you would find it was absolutely terrifying, bringing you very close to the verge of madness, because a skillful teacher in this method reduces you to a shuddering state of total insecurity. I have watched this being done among people you would consider perfectly ordinary, normal Westerners, who thought they were just getting involved in a nice, abstract intellectual discussion. Finally the teacher, as the process goes on, discovers in the course of the discussion what are the fundamental premises to which every one of his students is clinging. What is the foundation of sanity? What do you base your life on? When he has found that out for each student, he destroys it. He shows you that you cannot found a way of life on that, that it leads you into all sorts of inconsistencies and foolishness. The student turns back to the teacher and says, "It's all very well for you to pull out all carpets from under my feet; what would you propose instead?" And the teacher says, "I don't propose anything." He's no fool. He doesn't put up something to be knocked down. But here you are; if you do not put up something to be knocked down, you cannot play ball with the teacher. You may say, "I don't need to." But on the other hand, there is something nagging you inside, saying that you do. So you go play ball with him, and he keeps knocking down whatever you propose, whatever you cling to.

This exercise produces in the individual a real traumatic state. People get acute anxiety that you would not expect if it were seen as nothing more than a very intellectual and abstract discussion. When it really gets down to it, and you find that you do not have a single concept you can really trust, it's the heebie-jeebies. But you are preserved from insanity by the discipline, by the atmosphere set up by the teacher, and by the fact that he seems perfectly happy without anything in the way of a concept to cling to. The student looks at him and says, "He seems to be all right; maybe I can be all right too." This gives a certain confidence, a certain feeling that all is not mad, because the teacher in his own way is perfectly normal.

are and how we exist is a hallucination. To feel oneself as a separate ego, a source of action and awareness entirely separate and independent from the rest of the world, locked up inside a bag of skin, is in the view of the East a hallucination. You are not a stranger on the earth who has come into this world as the result of a fluke of nature, or as a spirit from somewhere outside nature altogether. In your fundamental existence you are the total energy of this universe playing the game of being you. The fundamental game of the world is the game of hide-and-seek. The colossal reality, the unitary energy that is the universe, plays at being many: it manifests itself as all these particulars around us. This is the fundamental intuition of Hinduism, Buddhism, and Taoism.

Buddhism originated in northern India close to the area that is now Nepal, shortly after 600 B.C. A young prince by the name of Gautama Siddhartha became the man we call the Buddha. "Buddha" is a title based on the Sanskrit root *budh*, which means to be awake. A buddha is an individual who has awakened from the dream of life as we ordinarily take it to be and discovered who we truly are. This idea was not something new. There was already in the whole complex of Hinduism the idea of buddhas, of awakened people. Curiously, they are ranked higher than gods. According to the Hindus, even the gods or the angels—the devas—are still bound on the wheel of life, are still trapped within the rat race pursuit of success, pleasure, virtue (which originally meant strength), magical power, or other positives. They are under illusion—are bound to the wheel of life—because they still believe positive and negative are opposites and that either one can exist without the other. This is illusion. You only know what "to be" is by contrasting it with "not to be." The front of a coin implies the existence of the back. If you try to gain the positive and escape the negative, it is as if you were trying to arrange everything in a room so that all of it was up and nothing was down. You cannot do it; you have set yourself an absolutely insoluble problem.

The basis of life is unity. Most people think of blue and red as being at opposite ends of the spectrum, but when they come together in the color purple, they actually complete a circle. Purple is the mixture of red and blue. Similarly, all sensations, all feelings, all experiences, occupy a point on a circle of sensations. Everyone is constantly operating through all the possible variations of experience. You cannot have one point on the circle without also knowing all the others. Even if you wanted to have only your favorite color, purple, you still have to have blue and red because without them you cannot have purple.

Of course, behind all the various colors in the spectrum is white light. Behind everything that we experience, all our various sensations of sound, of color, of shape, of touch, there is also white light, but here I am using that phrase symbolically, not literally. Yet common to all sensation is this basic sense. If you explored your sensations and began reducing them to the basic sense, you would be on your way to reality, to that which underlies everything, the ground of being, the basic energy. To the extent that you realize this basic energy and know that you are identical with it, you transcend, overcome, and surpass the illusion that you are simply John Doe, Mary Smith, or whoever. The Buddha, the man who woke up, is regarded as one buddha among a potentiality of myriads of buddhas. Everybody can be a buddha. All people have in themselves the capacity to wake up from the illusion of being simply a separate individual.

Buddhist teachings are divided and subdivided into groups of precepts. We are going to look at the Four Noble Truths of Buddhism, within which we will also encounter the Three Signs of Being, the Eightfold Path, the Five Vows, and the Three Refuges. Numbered statements of this type make the doctrines of Buddhism easier to understand.

Before waking up to his buddha nature, Gautama Siddhartha practiced the various disciplines that were offered in the Hinduism of his time. He found them unsatisfactory, however, because they overemphasized asceticism, which required one to put up with as much pain as possible. There was a feeling at the time that if the problem of life is pain, let us suffer. This is the reason ascetics lie on beds of nails, hold a hand up forever, eat only one banana a day, renounce sex, and do other weird things. If they headed into pain, they believed, and did not become afraid but suffered as much as possible, they would overcome the problem of pain and set themselves free from anxiety. There is a certain sense to this. If you had absolutely no fear of pain, no anxieties, no hang-ups about it, how strong you would be! You would have ultimate courage.

But the Buddha was very subtle. He was really the first

historical psychologist, the first great psychotherapist. He saw that a person who is fighting pain, who is trying to get rid of pain, is still fundamentally afraid of it. Therefore the way of asceticism would not work, and equally, hedonism, the opposite of asceticism, would not work. Therefore the Buddha devised the doctrine that is called the Middle Way, that is neither ascetic nor hedonistic.

This doctrine is summed up in what are called the Four Noble Truths. The first Noble Truth is *duhkha*, which in a very generalized sense means suffering. You could as easily say it means chronic frustration. Life as lived by most people is duhkha. It is, in other words, an attempt to solve insoluble problems, to draw a square circle, to have light without dark or dark without light. The attempt to solve problems that are basically insoluble, and to work at them through your whole life, is duhkha.

Buddha went on to subdivide this first Noble Truth into the Three Signs of Being.

The first sign is duhkha itself, frustration.

The second is *anitya*, impermanence. Every manifestation of life is impermanent. Our quest to make things permanent, to straighten everything out and get it fixed, presents us with an impossible and insoluble problem, and therefore we experience duhkha, the sense of fundamental pain and frustration that results from trying to make impermanent things permanent.

The third Sign of Being is *anatman*. The word *atman* means "self." *Anatman* means "nonself." I have explained elsewhere—in talking about Hinduism—that the idea of the ego is a social institution with no physical reality. The ego is simply your symbol of yourself. Just as the word *water* is a noise that symbolizes a certain liquid reality without being it, so too the idea of the ego symbolizes the role you play, who you are, but it is not the same as your living organism. Your ego has absolutely nothing to do with the way you color your eyes, shape your body, or circulate your blood. That is the real you, and it is certainly not your ego, because you do not even know how it is done. So anatman means, first, that the ego is unreal; there isn't one.

This brings us to the second of the Four Noble Truths, which is called *trishna*. *Trishna* is a Sanskrit word and the root of our word *thirst*. It is usually translated "desire," but it is better translated as "clinging," "grabbing," or to use excellent modern American slang, "a hang-up."

That is exactly what trishna is: a hang-up. When a mother is so afraid that her children may get into trouble that she protects them excessively, and as a result prevents them from growing, that is trishna. When lovers cling to each other excessively and feel they have to sign documents that they will swear to love each other always, they are in a state of trishna. When you hold on to yourself so tightly that you strangle yourself, that is trishna.

The second Noble Truth leads back to the first: clinging is what makes for suffering. When you fail to recognize that this whole world is a phantasmagoria, an amazing illusion, a weaving of smoke, and you try to hold on to it, then you will suffer seriously.

Trishna is itself based on *avidya*. Avidya is ignorance, and it means to ignore or overlook. We notice only what we think noteworthy, and so we ignore all kinds of things. Our vision of reality is highly selective; we pick out a few things and say that they are the universe. In the same way, we select and notice the figure rather than the background. Ordinarily, for instance, when I draw a circle on the blackboard, people see a ball, a circle, or a ring. But I have drawn a wall with a hole in it. You see? Similarly, we think we can have pleasure without pain. We want pleasure, the figure, and do not realize that pain is the background. Avidya is this state of restricted consciousness, or restricted attention. Bound by that state, we move through life, concentrating on one extreme or another, unaware of the fact that "to be" implies "not to be," and vice versa.

The third Noble Truth is called *nirvana*. This word means "exhale." You know that breath is life, and the Greek word *pneuma* conveys this same idea. It can mean either breath or spirit. In the Book of Genesis, when God had made the clay figurine that was later to be Adam, He breathed the breath of life into its nostrils and it became alive. Life is breath; but if you hold your breath you will lose your life. He who would save his life must lose it. Breathe in, in, in, get as much life as you can, and if you cling to it, you lose it. So nirvana means to breathe out: it is a great sigh of relief. Let the breath of life go because it will come back to you if you do. But if you do not let it go you will suffocate. A person in the state of nirvana is in a state of exhalation. Let go, don't cling, and you will be in the state of nirvana.

I reemphasize that I am not preaching to you about what you ought to do with your life. I am simply pointing out the state of affairs of the world as it is. There is no moralism in this whatsoever. If you put your hand into a fire, you will get burned. It is all right to get burned if you want to, but if it so happens that you do not want to get burned, then don't put your hand in a fire. It is the same if you do not want to be in a state of anxiety. It is perfectly all right to be anxious, if you like to be anxious. Buddhism never hurries anyone. It says, "You've got all eternity to live in various forms, therefore you do not have just one life in which to avoid eternal damnation. You can go running around the wheel in the rat race just as long as you want, so long as you think it's fun. And if there comes a time when you no longer think it's fun to be anxious, you don't have to continue." Someone who disagrees with this may say, "We ought to engage the forces of evil in battle and put this world to right, and arrange everything in it so that everything is good and nothing is bad." Try it, please. It is perfectly okay to try. And if you discover that these attempts are futile, you can then let go. You can give up clinging. Relax in that way and you will be in the state of nirvana. You will become a buddha. Of course, that will make you a rather astonishing person, although you may be subtle about it and disguise your buddhahood so that you will not get people mixed up.

The Buddha explained that his doctrine or method was a raft, sometimes called a *yana*, meaning a vehicle or conveyance. When you cross a river on a raft and you get to the other shore, you do not pick up the raft and carry it on your back. People who are hooked on religion are always on the raft. They are going back and forth and back and forth on the raft. The clergyman tends to become a ferryman who is always on the raft and never gets over to the other shore. There is something to be said for that, of course. How else are we to get the raft back to the first shore to bring over more people? Somebody has to volunteer to make the return journey. But one must realize that the real objective is to get the people across and set them free. If you dedicate yourself to ferrying people across, do not ask them to come back on the raft with you. People must not think that the raft is the goal; they must understand that it is simply a conveyance to the other shore, which is the real goal. When clergymen say, "We would like your pledge, your voluntary contribution," and nobody knows how much money to give, that is attachment to the idea of the raft.

We come now to the fourth Noble Truth, which is called *marga*. This word means "path." The way of Buddhism is often called the Noble Eightfold Path because of the eight methods or practices that are components of this last noble truth. These eight steps can be divided into three phases. They are not sequential and so do not need to be followed in any particular order. They are described by the word *samyak*, which, though it is usually translated as meaning "right," is actually the same, really, as our word *sum*: total, complete, all-inclusive. We might also use the word *integrated*—as when we say a person has integrity, is all of a piece, is not divided against himself—as a synonym for samyak.

The first phase of the eightfold path of the fourth Noble Truth consists of three components: right view, right consideration, and right speech. Right view, *samyak drishti*, is related to *samyak darshan*, which means a point of view, or a viewing. When you go to visit a great guru or teacher to have darshan, you look at him and offer your reverence to him. Darshan has many senses, but it means, simply, to view, or to look at the view.

As an example of right view, let us consider the right view of the constellation called the Big Dipper. When we look out from our specific, earthly point in space, it seems that the stars that form the Big Dipper must naturally form it, and always will. But imagine looking at them from somewhere else in space altogether. Those stars would not look like a dipper. They would be in an altogether different position relative to each other. What is the true relationship of those stars, then? There isn't one? Or else you could say that the true view of those stars would be their relationship when looked at from all points of view simultaneously. That would be the truth. But there is no such thing as the truth. The world, in other words, does not exist independently of those who witness it. Its existence derives from the existence of a relationship between the world and its witnesses. So if there are no eyes in this world, the sun doesn't make any light, nor do the stars. That which is, is a relationship. You can, for example, prop up two sticks by leaning them against each other. They will stand, but only by depending on each other. Take one away and the other falls. So in Buddhism it is taught that everything in this universe depends on everything else.

This is called the Doctrine of Mutual Interdependence. Everything hangs on you and you hang on everything, just as the two sticks support each other. This idea is conveyed in the symbol of Indra's net. Imagine a multidimensional spider's web covered with dewdrops. Every dewdrop contains the reflection of all the other dewdrops, and in each reflected dewdrop are the reflections of all the other dewdrops in that reflection, and so on, ad infinitum. That is the image of the Buddhist conception of the universe. The Japanese call that *ji ji muge*. *Ji* means a thing, event, or happening. *Muge* means "no separation." So, between happening and happening there is no separation: ji ji muge.

The second phase of the fourth Noble Truth has to do with action. It consists of three more paths: the paths of right action, right livelihood, and right effort. The Buddhist idea of ethics is based on expediency. If you are engaged in the way of liberation and you want to clarify your consciousness, your actions must be consistent with that goal. To this end, every Buddhist takes comfort in three refuges and makes five vows.

The Three Refuges are the Buddha; the dharma, or doctrine; and the sangha, or the fellowship of all those who are on the way. The Five Precepts are to undertake to abstain from taking life, from taking what is not given, from exploiting the passions, from falsifying speech, and from being intoxicated.

If you kill people you have to become involved in the consequences of that action. If you steal you have to suffer attachment to the consequences of that action. If you exploit your passions you must pay the consequences of that. A lot of people who suffer from obesity are trying simply to fill their empty psyche by stuffing themselves with food, but it is the wrong cure. If you start lying, you will become involved with the consequences of that action. Speech will collapse. So these five precepts represent a purely practical and utilitarian approach to morality.

The last phase of the Eightfold Path concerns the mind, or its state of consciousness, and has to do with what we would ordinarily call meditation. In this phase are the two final aspects of the path, the seventh and eighth. They are called *samyak smriti* and *samyak samadhi*.

Smriti means recollection or mindfulness. The word *re-collect* means to gather together what has been scattered. The opposite of "remember" is obviously "dismember." What has been chopped up and scattered becomes re-membered. In the Christian scheme—"Do this in remembrance of me"—the Christ has been sacrificed and chopped up, and the mass is a ritual of remembrance. One of the old liturgies says that the wheat that has been scattered all over the hills and then grows is gathered again into the bread, i.e., re-membered. In the Hindu view the world is regarded as the result of the dismemberment of the self, the *brahman*, the godhead. The one has been dismembered into the many. So remembrance means to realize that each single member of the many is really the one; that is re-collection.

You can think of this in another way. It is really the same way, but I will not explain exactly how. I will leave you with a few puzzles. This other way to be recollected is to be completely here and now.

There was a wise old boy who used to give lectures on

these things and he would get up and not say a word. He would just look at the audience and examine every person individually, and everyone would start to feel uncomfortable. He wouldn't say anything but would just look at everyone. Then he would suddenly shout, "WAKE UP! You're all asleep."

Are you here, recollected? Most people aren't. They are bothering about yesterday and wondering what they are going to do tomorrow, and they are not all here. That is a definition of sanity, to be all here. To be recollected is to be completely alert and available for the present, which is the only place you are ever going to be in. Yesterday does not exist. Tomorrow never comes. There is only today. A great Sanskrit invocation says, "Look to this day, for it is life. In its brief course lies all the realities of our existence. Yesterday is but a memory. Tomorrow is only a vision. Look well then to this day."

Beyond smriti, recollectedness, being all here, comes the last step of the Eightfold Path, samyak samadhi. Samyak samadhi is integrated consciousness; in it there is no separation between knower and the known, subject and object. You are what you know.

We think ordinarily that we are witnesses to a constantly changing panorama of experience from which we, as the knowers of this experience, stand aside and watch. We think of our minds as a kind of tablet on which experience writes a record. Eventually experience, by writing so much on the tablet, wears it out, scratches it away, and then we die. But actually there is no difference between the knower and the known. I cannot explain this to you in words; you can only find it out for yourself. When I say, "I see a sight; I feel a feeling," I am being redundant. "I see" implies the sight. "I feel" implies the feeling. Do you hear sounds? No, you just hear. Or else you can say simply that there are sounds; either way of expressing it will do. If you thoroughly investigate the process of experiencing, you will find that the experience is the same as the experiencer. This is the state of samadhi.

I suggested before that the organism and the environment are a single behavioral process. Now I will put it another way: the knower and the known are the same. You, as someone who is aware—along with all that you are aware of—are a single process. That is the state of samadhi.

You get to the samadhi state by the practice of meditation. Virtually every Buddha figure is seen in the posture of meditation, sitting quietly, aware of all that is going on without commenting on it, without thinking about it. When you cease categorizing, verbalizing, talking to yourself, the difference between knower and known, self and other, simply vanishes. What is the difference, anyway? Can you point to the thing that makes my fingers different from each other? There is no thing called difference. The idea of difference is an abstraction. It just does not exist in the physical world.

This is not to say, however, that my fingers are all the same. They are neither different nor the same. Difference and sameness are ideas. You cannot point to an idea. You cannot put your finger on it. This is what Buddhists mean when they say the world is basically *sunya*, empty, a void. Everything is sunya. You cannot catch the world in a conceptual net any more than you can catch water in a net. Sunya does not mean that the world itself and the energy of the world are nothing, however. It means that no concept of the world is valid. No ideas or beliefs or doctrines or systems or theories can contain the universe.

If you "exhale," then, if you let go of conceptions, you will be in the state of nirvana, for no reason that anybody can explain. When you enter that state there will well up from within you what the Buddhists call *karuna*, or compassion. This is the sense that you are not separate from everybody else but that everybody else is suffering as you are. It is a tremendous sense of solidarity with all other beings. The person who reaches nirvana does not withdraw from the world, therefore, but comes back from samadhi into it and its difficulties and all the problems of life renewed and filled with compassion for everyone.

This is the secret of the Middle Way: you cannot be saved alone because you are not alone. You are not an isolated point on a circle. You are not one extreme point on a spectrum, separate from any of the other points. You are the whole cosmos.

CHAPTER THREE

Religion of No-Religion

P reviously I have discussed the bodhisattva doctrine in Mahayana Buddhism and have related it to the two great tendencies in Indian spirituality: antiworldliness—or otherworldliness—and world affirmation. I have shown that the highest kind of buddha is in a certain way a non-buddha.

The highest kind of buddha is like an ordinary person. This comes out clearly in various tendencies in Zen. For example, all the paintings characteristic of Zen Buddhism in the Chinese and Japanese traditions are secular. They have a nonreligious atmosphere about them, whereas the paintings of the older Japanese Shingon and Tendai sects are religious paintings; you can tell at once that the subject matter of these paintings is religious. But with Zen painting the way of dealing with philosophical or spiritual themes is secular.

This ordinary quality is apparent in the works of Sengai, a Zen monk from seventeenth-century Japan. When an artist like Sengai paints the Buddha, there is something slightly humorous about the image of the Buddha. He wears his halo over one ear, and there is an informality to him, a slight raffishness. This style comes from China, from those great Sung dynasty artists like Liangkai, who painted the sixth patriarch of Zen chopping bamboo, looking like an unkempt country oaf. The greatest Zen painting has as its subject matter themes that are not really religious at all. It uses pine branches, rocks, bamboos, and grasses, and you would never know that these were religious icons.

Likewise in poetry, which we will go into more extensively later. A superb expression of Zen poetry is derived from the Chinese poet Layman Pang, who says, "Wondrous action, supernatural power, chopping wood and carrying water." That is a little bit too religious for Zen taste, however. Preferable is Bashō's famous poem, "The old pond; a frog jumps in. Plop." "Plop" is the best English translation for the Japanese *mizu no oto*, which means, literally, "the water's sound." That is a very high-style Zen poem, because it has nothing in it about religion. There is another poem by Bashō that says, "When the lightning flashes, how admirable, he who does not think life is fleeting." The flash of lightning is a Buddhist cliché for the transiency of the world, that life goes by and disappears as fast as a flash of lightning. How admirable, the poet is saying, not to be trapped by a cliché.

All religious comments about life eventually become clichés. Religion is always falling apart and promoting lip service and imitation. The imitation of Christ, for instance, is a perfect example. It is a terrible idea because everyone who imitates Christ becomes a kind of fake Jesus. In the same way, there are all kinds of imitation Buddhas in Buddhism, not only sitting on gilded wooden altars but sitting around in the monasteries, too. One might say that the highest kind of religious or spiritual attainment shows no sign that it is religious or spiritual. As a metaphor for this, there is in Buddhism the idea of the tracks of birds in the sky. Birds do not leave tracks, and so the way of the enlightened man is like the tracks of a bird in the sky. As a Chinese poem says, "Entering the forest, he does not disturb a blade of grass. Entering the water, he does not make a ripple."

In other words, there is no sign about the spiritually advanced to indicate that they are self-consciously religious. Nor are they self-conscious about giving the world no sign of their advanced spiritual state. They are not like Protestants, self-consciously proud of their simplicity, criticizing the Catholics with their rituals. Historically, however, the real reason Protestants think Catholic rituals are insincere is that they are expensive. Protestantism started in the burgher cities of Europe, places like Augsburg, Hamburg, and Geneva, where the merchant class, who were the foundation of the bourgeoisie, were annoyed because every time a saint's day came around all their employees got a day off to attend mass. There were so many of these nuisance holy days, as well as numerous contributions assessed by the church to pay for masses for the dead and to buy one's way out of purgatory, that the merchants found this very uneconomical. The priests were getting the money instead of them, so they decried as unbiblical, irreligious, and wasteful all the finery of the Catholic religion, and sought a plain and simple alternative. In the course of time it became a sign of being genuinely religious to avoid rituals and colorful clothing and splendor in churches, and to be as ordinary as possible. But this is not an example of the way real religion gives no sign of being religious, because this simplicity and absence of ritual was itself a sign of piety; it was a way of advertising how spiritual one was.

The true bodhisattva does not leave a track of any kind, either by being overtly religious or by being overtly nonreligious.

But how can you be neither religious nor nonreligious? That is the great test. How can you avoid that trap of being one or the other? It is similar to the question, Are you a theist or an atheist? The theist is caught by God, and the idea of God or the belief in God, but the atheist is equally caught. If, for instance, an atheist is an atheist because he cannot stand the idea that God is watching him all the time—that there is an all-seeing eye prying into his most private life—then he is as trapped by his opposition to God as a theist is caught by his idea of God. Atheists who advertise their disbelief in God are very pious people. Nobody believes in God like an atheist: "There is no God, and I am His prophet." The true bodisattva state is very difficult to pin down. It is neither supremely religious nor blatantly secular. It is a very subtle state. Everyone misses the point. Even people who think that the height of Buddhism or Zen is to be perfectly ordinary have still missed the point.

There is an element of the nonreligious in the art, the painting, and the poetry that has been inspired by the appearance of ordinariness in Buddhist saints. Nevertheless, there is something about the way in which this nonreligious subject matter is handled that stops you. You know there is something strange about it. This is how I first became interested in Oriental philosophy. I had an absolute fascination for Chinese and Japanese secular painting— the landscapes, the treatment of flowers and grasses and bamboos. There was something about that treatment that struck me as astonishing, even though the subject matter was extremely ordinary. Even as a child I had to find out what the strange element in those bamboos and grasses was. I was, of course, being taught by those painters to see grass, but there was something else in their paintings that I could never put my finger on. That "something else" was this thing that I will call the religion of no-religion. It is the supreme attainment of a buddha: it cannot be detected; it leaves no trace.

Some of you have seen the paintings of the Ten Stages of Spiritual Ox-herding. There are two sets of these paintings: a heterodox sequence and an orthodox. In the heterodox sequence, as the man catches the ox, the ox becomes progressively whiter, until in the end it disappears altogether. The last picture is of an empty circle. But the orthodox set of paintings does not end with the empty circle. The image of the empty circle is followed by two others. After the man has attained the state of emptiness—the state of no attachment to any spiritual or psychological or moral crutch—there follow two more steps. The first is called "Returning to the Origin." It is represented by a tree beside a stream. The last is called "Entering the City With Gift-bestowing Hands." It shows a picture of the Buddha Putai, in Japanese known as Hotei, who has an enormous belly, big ears, and carries around a colossal bag. What do you think his bag has in it? Trash, wonderful trash. Everything that children love. Things that everybody else has thrown away, and thought of as valueless, this Buddha collects and gives away to children. The saying is, "He goes on his way without following the steps of the ancient sages. His door is closed"—that is, the door of his house—"and no glimpses of his interior life are to be seen."

In other words, when you erect a building, you have to put all kinds of scaffolding up. This shows that building is going on. When the building is complete, however, the scaffolding is taken down. The scaffolding is religion. To open a door, as they say in Zen, you may need to knock on it with a brick. But when the door is open, you do not carry the brick inside. Similarly, to cross a river you need a boat, but when you have reached the other side, you do not pick up the boat and carry it across the land on your back. The brick, the boat, the scaffolding, all represent religious technology, or method, and in the end these are all to disappear. The saint will not be found in church. However, do not take what I say literally. The saint can perfectly readily go to church without being sullied by church. It is ordinary people who too frequently come out of church stinking of religion.

A disciple once asked a great Zen master, "Am I making progress?"

He said, "You're doing all right, but you have a trivial fault."

"What is that?"

"You have too much Zen."

"Well," the student said, "when you're studying Zen, don't you think it's very natural to be talking about it?"

The master said, "When it is like an ordinary conversation, it is much better."

Another monk who was standing by, listening to this exchange, said to the master, "Why do you so dislike talking about Zen?"

The master replied, "Because it turns one's stomach."

What did he mean when he said that it is better to talk about Zen when it is like an ordinary, everyday conversation? When the old master Joshu was asked, "At the end of the present epoch of history, when everything will be destroyed in fire, one thing will remain. What will it be?" Joshu replied, "It's windy again this morning."

In Zen when you are asked a question about religion you reply in terms of the secular. When you are asked about something secular, you reply in terms of religion: "What is the eternal nature of the self?" "It is windy again this morning."

When a student asked his master to hand him a knife, the master handed it to him blade first. The student said,

"Please give me the other end." "What would you do with the other end?" the master asked. Do you see? The disciple started out with the ordinary and suddenly found himself involved in a metaphysical problem. But if he'd started out with the metaphysical, he would have found himself involved with the knife.

To go deeply into the religion of no-religion we have to understand what might be called the final, ultimate attainment of Mahayana Buddhist philosophy. This is contained in a school of thought that is called in Chinese *Huayen*, and in Japanese *Kegon*. Kegon is the intellectual foundation for Zen. There was a great Chinese master by the name of Tsungmi, or Shumitsu in Japanese, who was simultaneously a Zen master and the fifth patriarch of the Chinese Huayen sect. *Hua* means "flower"; *yen*, "garland." The Garland of Flowers is a lengthy Sanskrit sutra called the *Avatamsaka*; in Japanese it is called the *Kegon-kyo*. One subject of this vast and visionary sutra is what are called the four dharma worlds, and I will explain what these four worlds are.

First there is a level of being that is called *ji* in Japanese, *shih* in Chinese. This is the world of things and events. It is what you might call the commonsense world, the everyday world that our senses normally record. The Chinese character *shih* has a multiplicity of meanings. It can mean a thing or an event, and it can mean important business. It can mean affectation, putting something on or showing off. A person who is a master in Zen is called *buji*, which means "no business, no affectation, nothing special." A poem says, "On Mount Lu there is misty rain, and the

River Zhe is at high tide. When you have not been there, your heart is filled with longing. But when you have been there and come back, it was nothing special. Misty rain on a mountain. A river at high tide."

This "nothing special" is buji. We feel that when something is nothing special it must be ordinary. But buji does not mean ordinary. It means, paradoxically—to our ears—that the mountain and river were nothing special in the same way that individuals with no religion can be the most truly religious of all. They are not just common, ignorant people, though they may appear that way. You have to know what they know to recognize them for who and what they are. The "nothing special" of buji means that the inner specialness does not stick out like a sore thumb. So the world of ji is in general the world of particulars, the world of multiplicity. It is the world we ordinarily feel we are living in, and it is the first of the four dharma worlds.

The second dharma world is called the world of *ri* in Japanese; in Chinese, *li*. In Chinese this character means the markings in jade, the grain in wood, the fiber in muscle; the organic principle of order. In the Huayen philosophy, the word li or ri means the universal that underlies all particulars, the unity underlying all multiplicity, the unitive principle, as distinct from shih, or ji, which is the differentiation principle.

When you first see into the nature of the world, you start from ji. You begin by noticing all the particular things in the world and by being baffled by their multiplicity, and by dealing with the multiplicity of things. But as you progress in understanding, you become aware of the relationship each thing has to the other, and eventually you see the unity that lies behind them. The multiplicity of the world dissolves into unity.

At this point you encounter a problem. You can see the world as a unity and you can see it as a multiplicity. But how the devil are you to put those two visions together? If you are to be a practical success in business, in family life, and so on, you have to pay attention to the world of particulars. It is particulars that matter. You have to know chalk from cheese. But if you become a saint, a monk, or a hermit—or perhaps even a poet or an artist—then you will have to forget about the practical matters and contemplate the unity, the secret meaning underlying all events. But then all the practical people are going to say, "You're falling down on the job. You're avoiding life." They feel that the world of particulars is the only real world. But the saint will say, "Your particulars are not real. You make a success of things, but it is only a temporary success. You think you're an important person, you're really contributing to human life, but actually your success will last for only a few years and then you will fall apart like everybody else. When you're dead, where will your success be then?" From the standpoint of the person who concentrates on the underlying unity of the world, such success isn't real.

To solve the problem of unifying the visions of the first two dharma worlds, we have to go to the third of these worlds, which is called *ri ji muge*. The name of this world is formed from the names of the first two, combined with *muge*, meaning "no block." It means that between ri and ji there is no blockage; there is no obstruction between the world's unity and its particulars. The world of the universal and the world of particulars are not incompatible. To demonstrate this, let's take two very different things—for example, shape and color—and see how they can be united. A shape can never be a color, a color can never be a shape, but shape and color can be joined in a single object. Think of color and shape as the first two dharma worlds. They can be united in an object—such as a circle—to form, metaphorically, the third dharma world.

The properly rounded person is an embodiment of the third dharma world, is both spiritual and material, is both otherworldly and worldly. This is the supreme attainment of a human being, to be fully both worldly and otherworldly, to avoid the extreme of one-sidedness. The person who is just a materialist ends up by being very boring. You can live the successful life of the world and own every kind of material refinement, have the most beautiful home, the most delicious food, the most marvelous yachts and cars, but if you have no touch of the mystical about you, material success will eventually become perfectly boring, and you will get tired of it. On the other hand, there are people who are purely spiritual, who live in a dry world where all luxury has been scrubbed away, and they are very intense people. When you are in the presence of an excessively spiritual person, you feel inclined to sit on the edge of your chair. You are not at ease.

It is always puzzling to people brought up in a Western environment that, in the East, great spiritual people are often quite sensuous. They cannot be materialists in the ordinary sense, but neither can they be the kind of straightforward sensualists who use the world purely for their own pleasure. The world is too wonderful for that. Human beings, for instance, are too marvelous to be treated as merely sensual objects. A person may indeed be very sexual, but they are also, in addition, so wonderful that one has to stop and delve into the wholeness of their marvelous personality, as well as into their sensual qualities.

A problem with sensuality keeps recurring in the West. For instance, one goes to a church with a fine clergyman who is idolized, the very exemplar of life, and then suddenly there develops a frightful scandal; he has an affair with his secretary, for instance.

When this happens, a Westerner tends to think that all is lost, the faith has been sold out, and everything is going to wrack and ruin, all because the clergyman was not purely spiritual but also had a hidden sensual side. In the West we frequently see this kind of one-sidedness—of excessive materialism or spirituality—because in our world we tend to make the spiritual and the material mutually exclusive. But in the third dharma world of ri ji muge, we see that there is no separation between the spiritual and the material.

The attainment of this world might seem to be the highest possible achievement. But there is still one more world beyond it, which is called *ji ji muge*. Suddenly ri, the world of unity, has disappeared, but between ji and ji—particular and particular—there is still no obstruction. Between one event and any other event or events there is no mutual exclusiveness, nothing that need be united with an underlying unity. This is the highest doctrine of Mahayana Buddhism. It is the idea of the mutual inter-penetration of all things, or the mutual interdependence of all things. Its symbol is Indra's net, the principle of which is elaborated in the *Avatamsaka sutra*.

Imagine at dawn a multidimensional spider's web cov-ered with dew, a vast spider's web that is the whole cosmos. It exists in four, five, six, or more dimensions, and at every intersection of web are rainbow-colored jewels of dew on which are reflected every other drop of dew, and therefore also the reflections of all the other drops of dew, and also the reflections of the reflections, and so on, ad infinitum.

This is the Mahayana vision of the world. No thing, no event, can exist without every other thing or event. Every event implies all events; every event—the total uni-verse, past, present, future—depends on every particular event or thing. It is easy to say, "I depend on the universe. There could be no me unless there was everything else." It is harder to see the corollary, that the whole universe depends on you. "After all," you might say, "before I was born the universe was here, and after I die I'm sure it will go on. How can it be said, then, that the whole universe depends on me?" Very simply: without your parents you would not have come into being. For you to exist it was necessary for your parents to exist. That necessity doesn't change when they die. Therefore you depend on your parents even when they have gone. In the same way the universe will still depend on you, on your having been here, even when you disappear. And if you have not yet been born, it depends on your future arrival here. The fact that you exist tells us something about the kind of universe we're living in: it once produced you. You are a symptom of the kind of universe we're living in, just as an apple is a symptom of a certain kind of tree. It tells us something about that tree, what its function is. A world that produces a John Doe, who is nobody in particular, who is not even remembered by anybody, nevertheless depends on him, despite his obscurity, for its existence, just as it depends equally on every fruit fly, every gnat, every vibration of every gnat's wing, on every last electron in every last gnat's wing—on every one of its manifestations—however brief those manifestations may be.

What I am saying is that everything that exists implies everything else, and all those other things, collectively, in their totality—which we call the universe—in turn imply each individual object and event. That is the meaning of Indra's net. When you have a chain and you pick up a link, all the other links come up with it, and this is called in Zen, "to take up a blade of grass and use it as a golden Buddha, sixteen feet high." There is no such thing as a single, solitary event. The only possible single event is all events whatsoever. That could be regarded as the only possible atom; the only possible single thing is everything. The manifestations of the universe that we call things all imply each other. We know what we are only in relation to what we are not. We know the sensation of the self only in relation to a sensation of the other. The self implies the other as the back implies the front. However short or long it may be, everything depends on your life. If you did not happen, nothing would happen. The whole world bears your signature, and it would not be the same world if you weren't in it.

Have you heard of the pathetic fallacy? This was a nineteenth-century idea that asserted that it is false and illegitimate to project human feelings onto the world. The wind in the pine trees is not sighing; you are projecting sighing onto the sound. The sun is not happy; you are projecting your own happiness onto the shining sun. The sun has no feeling; the sun is not human. The wind has no feeling; it is not human. The poet may say, "The moon doth with delight look around her when the heavens are bare." But the logician will answer: "No, it is the poet who is looking around with delight at the moon in the bare heavens." How awful. If that were true, it would be better to ban poetry from the world. But actually the moon does look around with delight when the poet does, because the same world that manifests itself as the moon also manifests itself as the poet. They go together. A world where there is a moon implies a world where there is a poet. A world where there is a poet implies a world where there is a moon. So, through the agency of the poet, the moon can in fact be said to look around with delight. You cannot separate poet and moon without destroying the universe, any more than you can separate head and feet without destroying the body. In that sense then this whole world is a human world. We should not take seriously the silly idea of the pathetic fallacy, which says that outside our skins everything is inhuman—a mass of dumb and blind forces—and that only inside the skin is there a human world. All the world is human, and it depends not only on the existence of humanity in general but also on every individual in particular.

The whole world is covered, as it were, with your personal signature. However, the moment you see yourself as central to the existence of the universe, you will suddenly see the obverse of this as well: that your particular personality is nothing at all without the existence of everything else and everybody else. In order for me to be Alan Watts I need every single other human being, including their uncontrollable otherness. They are going to be themselves whatever I do, and I depend on all their differences from me, and they all depend, likewise, on my differences from them. So I am in a very funny position. The moment I would be egoless and say, "I am nothing without you," I find that I am the kingpin: they all depend on me. And when I get swell-headed about being the kingpin, I discover I am nothing at all without them. The moment you think you're in one state, that state transforms itself into its opposite. That is ji ji muge, the fourth dharma world. In it everybody is the boss and nobody is. The whole thing takes care of itself. In this sense the world is a colossal democracy, and every man, every nightingale, every snail, is king in this world and commoner at the same time. That's how it works.

There is no great king. In Hinduism they do have what is to us a very strange idea called *Ishvara*. This is the supreme personal god, the top being in the deva world. Many Buddhists also believe in such a god or ruler of the universe, but they think that he is lower than a buddha, because, like all gods and all angels, but unlike a buddha, he is still subject to the round of being and will eventually dissolve into nothing. This is a very curious idea to our minds. Buddhists believe in this kind of supreme god, but they do not believe that that god is particularly important. There are no shrines in Buddhism to Ishvara.

So it is this idea of the mutual interpenetration and interdependence of all things that is the philosophical basis for Zen as a practical, nonintellectual way of life. Because the most ordinary events or things—charcoal brazier, mat, soup for dinner, sneezing, washing hands, going to the bathroom—all imply, despite their separateness, the unity of the universe. That is why Zen people use ordinary events to demonstrate cosmic and metaphysical principles. They do not rationalize it in this way, however. To see infinity in a grain of sand and eternity in an hour is still ri ji muge, not ji ji muge. Ji ji muge is when you offer somebody the grain of sand without thinking about eternity. There is no difference between the grain of sand and eternity. You do not have to think about eternity as something implied by the grain of sand. The grain of sand is eternity. In exactly the same way, our sitting here at this moment is not something different from nirvana. We are in nirvana sitting here exactly as we are. You do not have to make any philosophical comment on the grain of sand or on our sitting here. Comment is unnecessary. Such comment is called "legs on a snake" or "beard on a eunuch." Putting legs on a snake embarrasses the snake; a eunuch does not need a beard. In our idiom we say, "Don't gild the lily." Zen says, "Do not put frost on top of snow."

All specifically religious activity is "legs on a snake."

CHAPTER FOUR

Buddhism As Dialogue

I want to proceed now with a discussion of the particular subset of Mahayana Buddhism that is known as Zen Buddhism.

Zen plays a little game with you. Whenever I or somebody like D. T. Suzuki talks about Zen, all the others say that because we're talking about it we do not understand it. In the words of Lao-tzu, "Those who know do not say; those who say do not know," and though he said that, he wrote a book of eighty chapters or so to explain the Tao and the *te*, its power. We can't help ourselves; we've got to talk. Human beings are chatterboxes. When we have something on our minds, we have to talk about it, even if we can't say what we mean.

Poetry is the great language. It is the art of saying what cannot be said. Every poet knows that he is trying to describe the indescribable. Every poet knows that nothing is describable. Whether you take some sort of ineffable mystical experience at one extreme, or an ordinary rusty nail at the other, nothing is really describable. In the words of the famous Count Korzybski, "Whatever you say something is, it isn't."

There used to be a professor at Northwestern who would produce a matchbook in front of his class and say, "What is this?" The students would say, "A match-book." And he would say, "No, no, no. 'Matchbook' is a noise. Is this a noise? What is it really?" And to answer this, he would throw it at them. That is what it was.

So nothing can really be described, and yet we all know perfectly well what we mean when we talk. If you have shared an experience with somebody else, then of course you can talk about it. We can all talk about fire and air and water and wood because we know what they are, and there is no mystery. In the same way, something so esoteric as Zen can be discussed. Zen people play games or little tricks, however, and test each other. I remember the first time I met Paul Reps, who wrote that lovely book *Zen Flesh, Zen Bones*. He said to me, "You've written quite a number of books by now, you must think you're pretty fancy." I said, "I haven't said a word." This is simply a Zen game where people feel each other out. A poem says, "When two Zen masters meet each other on the road, they need no introduction; thieves recognize one another instantaneously."

If I were to give you a truly proper and educated talk about Zen, I would gather you around and sit here in silence for five minutes and leave. This would be a much more direct exposition of it than what I am going to do instead, which is to talk about it. I am afraid that you would feel disappointed and somewhat cheated if I just left after five minutes of silence though.

The word *zen* is the Japanese way of mispronouncing the Chinese word *chan* which, in turn, is the Chinese way of mispronouncing the Sanskrit word *dhyana*. *Dhyana* is a very difficult if not impossible word to translate into English. It has been called meditation, but *meditation* in English generally means sitting quietly and thinking about something, and that is not what Zen is. *Contemplation* might come a little nearer if you use the word in the very technical sense that is still used among Catholic mystics. Contemplation, as we normally use the word, has a sense of inactivity, a sense of not doing anything but being completely still and passive. Zen, however, is something highly active. So we really do not have an English word for dhyana, Chan, or Zen.

But I would say that we do know what Zen is, because we do all sorts of things every day of our lives in the spirit of Zen. For example, most Americans have driven cars since they were teenagers and are very expert drivers. And when they drive a car, they do not think about it; they are one with the car. Similarly, an expert horse rider is one with the horse. When you watch a good cowboy or cavalry rider, he's glued to the horse, almost like a centaur. As the horse moves, he moves. Which is in control? Is the horse riding the man or the man riding the horse? You really don't know. The same is true when you have an excellent dancing partner; who leads? Who follows? It seems as if you are one body and you move together. That is Zen.

In a wider sense, when a person does not react to life, on the one hand, or tries to dominate it, on the other, but allows the internal world of his own organism and the external world of other people and other things to move together as if they were one and the same motion, that is Zen. So you could say in a very simple way that the real concern of Zen is to realize—not merely rationally but in one's bones—that the world inside your skin and the world outside your skin are all one world and one being, one self. And you are it.

Once you know that, you have abolished all the problems that arise when you feel that you are a stranger in the world, set down in the middle of an alien world, surrounded by lifeless galaxies that are inhabited by strange people. This whole sense of estrangement from a foreign world is overcome in Zen.

I will illustrate this, before we go into Zen in any kind of technical way, with a few rather superficial but nevertheless significant facts out of Japanese culture and the place of Zen in it. Japanese culture is extraordinarily ritualistic. There is a right way of doing everything, a good form, a proper style. Nowhere is this more apparent than in such practices as the tea ceremony or flower arrangement, or in knowing how to dress or how to organize a formal dinner. The punctiliousness and skill of these people in doing these things is quite remarkable. But to the same degree that they are very skillful at doing these things, they are very worried about them. For example, the whole question of bringing presents to somebody is of great concern. Have they given us more than we have given them? Did we remember this or that occasion? These questions weigh very heavily on the Japanese soul. The debt that you owe to your parents, the debt that you owe to your country and to your emperor, are immeasurable, infinite debts that never can be paid. These weigh very heavily. Therefore Japan—until the partial breakaway of modern youth, with its Westernized ideals—has had a very nervous culture, concerned about whether one is playing the ritual correctly.

A culture like that needs an outlet, a safety valve, and Zen provides just that. So when you meet a Japanese person who is thoroughly trained in Zen, he has a different kind of personality altogether when compared with his countryman who is not trained in Zen. His manners are not studiedly courteous, nor is he brusque, but he is simply at ease. He gives you his whole attention, so long as you give him your whole attention. If your attention starts wandering, though, he has work to do and promptly leaves. But so long as you are wanting to talk to him, he is there for you and for nobody else. He sits down, and he really sits, unworried about whether he ought to be somewhere else. He is able to sit in one place with complete serenity. If you have half an idea that you ought to be worrying about something out in the garden, or that you ought to be cooking dinner, or that you ought to be down in your office, you cannot sit where you are. You are not really there. You are a kind of helium balloon that keeps wanting to wander off. But when you meet people connected with Zen you see they are grounded. Even the most neophyte, novice priest, has this atmosphere of knowing how to live in the present without being fidgety or giggly or worrying about whether he has done the right thing, and that is very much the Zen style.

Although Zen people do have a very exacting and demanding discipline, the function of this discipline is rather curious: it is to enable them to be comfortable. It is to enable them, for example, to be able to sleep on a concrete sidewalk on a cold, wet night and enjoy it. It is to enable them to be able to relax completely under any situation or hardship. Ordinarily, if you sit out in the cold, you will start shivering. This is because you will be resisting the cold, tightening your muscles against it. But Zen discipline teaches you to do something else, to take it easy, go with the cold, relax.

All those monks in monasteries in Japan are cold as hell in winter. And they simply sit there, most of the time. We would feel frozen to death and miserable, and would start coming down with influenza and pneumonia, but they simply relax and learn how to accept the cold. There is nothing about Zen discipline that is masochistic, however. It has nothing to do with the idea that you must beat your body because your body is bad because it is the creation of the devil. It simply teaches the disciple how to be comfortable under all circumstances. But all of this is rather incidental to the main question of Zen.

The Zen people, as you meet them and get to know

their personality style, are at ease in a culture that is not at ease but instead is chronically concerned with protocol. Japanese culture is a terribly self-conscious culture. Everybody is always watching themselves and having second thoughts about everything. This becomes tiresome. The discipline of Zen emerged out of this situation as a method for enabling students of Zen to act without watching themselves; to act unself-consciously, we would say. The Japanese are terrified of this kind of action, as are we. They, and we too, think, "If I don't watch myself constantly I will make a mistake. If I don't hold a club over my own head, I will cease to be civilized; I will become a barbarian. If I don't discipline myself and repress those passions of mine, I will become like the monk from Siberia who burst from his cell one day and devoured the father superior."

Our basic mistrust of our own spontaneity makes us wonder whether the Zen people are really spontaneous. If they do not plan and premeditate and hold clubs over themselves, won't they become very dangerous people socially? Won't they go out and rape their mothers and daughters, and murder their grandmothers to inherit their fortunes, and so forth? Zen people just do not do that, of course, and yet they really are perfectly spontaneous. To show how this can be, I will try to indicate how this discipline called Zen actually works. This will involve letting the cat out of the bag a little bit, but that cannot be helped.

Let us go back to what is fundamental to Buddhism. Buddhism is unlike Western religions in that it does not tell you anything. It does not require you to believe in anything. It is a dialogue. The teachings of Buddhism are nothing more than the opening phrases or exchanges in that dialogue.

Buddhism is a dialogue between a buddha and an ordinary man, or rather, between a buddha and another buddha who insists on defining himself as an ordinary man, thereby creating a problem. There is a saying that "anybody who goes to a psychiatrist ought to have his head examined." In exactly the same way, in the Buddhist culture, anybody who goes to a guru, a spiritual teacher, a Zen master, or whatever, ought to have his head examined. As the old Chinese master Tokusan put it, "If you ask any question, you get thirty blows with my stick. If you don't ask any question, you get thirty blows just the same." In other words, "What the hell are you doing here defining yourself as a student and me as a teacher?" You raise a problem when you do that, and in the Zen way of training, this problem is very clearly emphasized.

If you go to a Zen teacher and approach him in the traditional way, the first thing he will do is say, "I haven't anything to teach. Go away."

You may say, "What are these people doing around here? Aren't they your students?"

He will answer, "They are working with me. But unfortunately we are very poor these days. We don't have enough rice to go around. We can't make ends meet as it is. We cannot take on anybody else in this community."

So you have to insist on being taken in. Every postulant for Zen training assumes immediately that the teacher has given him the brush-off in order to test his sincerity. In other words, "If you really want this thing, you have got to work for it." That is not the real point. The point is that you have got to make such a fuss to get in that you cannot withdraw gracefully after having made such a fuss. You put yourself on the spot and define yourself as somebody needing help, or as somebody with a problem who needs a master in order to be helped out of the problem. In the old days—and it is still the rule today among the Zen monasteries of Japan—a postulant who wanted to come into a monastery had to sit outside the gate for five days, in a position of supplication, with head bowed down on the steps. The monks inside would let him in at night because they must give hospitality to any wandering monk, but he was expected not to sleep any of those five nights but to sit in meditation. You sit, and you sit, and you sit there, making a fool of yourself and saying, "I insist on being admitted into this monastery. I insist on learning the secret of the master here." The master has already told you that he does not have a secret and that he does not teach anything. But you insist that he does.

This is the situation of everyone who feels that life is a problem to be solved. Whether you seek to solve that problem through psychoanalysis, integration, salvation, or buddhahood, you define yourself in a certain way when you see life as a problem to be solved.

The real desire that everybody brings to these teachers can be stated in this way: "Teacher, I want to get one up on the universe. I feel I am a stranger in this world and that life is a problem. Having a body means that I am subject to disease and change and death. Having emotions and passions means that I am tormented by feelings I cannot help having, and yet it is not possible to act on those feelings without creating trouble. I feel trapped by this world and so I want to get the better of it. Is there some wise man around who is a master of life and who can teach me to cope with all this?" That is what everybody is looking for in a teacher: a savior who can show you how to cope with life. But the Zen teacher says, "I don't have any answers." Nobody believes that because he seems to be so confident when you look at him. You cannot believe that he has no answers, and yet the consistent teaching of Zen is that it has nothing to say and nothing to teach.

A great Chinese master of the Tang dynasty, called Linji in Chinese, or Rinzai in Japanese, said, "Zen is like using a yellow leaf to stop a child crying. A child is crying for gold and the father takes an autumn leaf that is yellow and calls it gold." He also said that it is like using an empty fist to deceive a child. You have a closed fist and you say to the child, "What have I got here?" And the child says, "Let me see!" You put your fist behind your back, and the child becomes more and more excited to know what the devil is inside that fist, and fights and fights and finally is practically in tears, and then suddenly you open the fist and there is nothing inside.

This is how it is for the person who is under the impression that life is a problem to be solved. The secret is dressed up in a big way: to know it is to be a buddha; it is to know the answer, to solve the problem, to get the message, to get the word, to be in control of fate and the world. Who wouldn't want that?

All these powers are projected on the Zen master: he is a buddha, a master of life. But if he is a master of life, the reason for that is that he has discovered the unreality of the whole problem of life. There is not life on the one hand and you on the other. You and life are the same. But you cannot tell people that and just by telling it get them to see it.

People who know that the earth is flat cannot be reasoned with. It is absolutely impossible to reason with people who believe that the Bible is the literal word of God. In the same way, we tend to know that we are each a separate "poor little me," and that we are in need of salvation or something. We know this is so, and if somebody says, "You are not really separate from life; your feeling of separateness is an illusion," that is all very nice—in theory—but we do not feel it.

So what will you do with a person who is convinced that the earth is flat? There is no way of reasoning with him. If it is for some reason important that he discover that the earth is round, you have got to play a game or trick on him. You tell him, "Great. The earth is flat. Let's go and look over the edge; wouldn't that be fun? Of course, if we are going to look over the edge of the earth, we must be very careful that we do not go around in circles or we will never get to the edge. So we must go along consistently westward, along a certain line of latitude. Then we will come to the edge of the earth." In other words, in order to convince a flat-earther that the world is round, you have to make him act consistently on his own proposition by making him go consistently westward in search of the edge of the world. When at last, by going consistently westward, he comes back to the place where he started, he will have been convinced that the earth is at least cylindrical, and he may then take it on faith that if he goes north along a line of longitude, he will again eventually return to his starting place. What you must do is make him persist in his folly. That is the whole method of Zen: to make people become consistent, perfect egotists, and so explode the illusion of the separate ego.

When you finally convince the Zen master that you are stupid enough to be accepted as a student—by persisting in defining yourself as someone with a problem that he can solve for you, even through he has warned you well in advance that he has nothing to teach—he will then say, "I will now ask you a question."

There are many ways of asking this question, but they all boil down to one common question, which is, "Who are you? You say you have a problem. You say you would like to get out of the sufferings of life and get one up on the universe. I want to know who is asking this question. Show me you."

The master may put the question like this: "Before your father and mother conceived you, what was your original nature?" And they add, "I want to be shown. I do not want a lot of ideas from you about who you are. I do not want to know who you are in terms of a social role, college degrees, professional qualifications, your name, your family. All that is the past. I want to see the genuine you as you are right now."

This is like saying to a person, "Don't be self-conscious.

I want you, right this minute, to be completely sincere." Nothing is better calculated to make a person incapable of sincerity. It is as when a child's relatives come, aunts and uncles, and the parents say, "Darling, come on now and show us how you have fun." The poor child is completely nonplussed and does not know what to do. You cannot have fun on demand.

The context in which a Zen master interviews his students is very formal; there he sits, sort of an enthroned tiger, definitely an authority figure. He is the last person you can be spontaneous with, because you feel that he knows you through and through.

There is a story about a man who has a fight with a bear, and the bear is a mind reader and always knows what moves the man is going to make. So the man can never conquer the bear unless he makes a move that he does not think about first. You get the same feeling about a Zen master: that he is absolutely aware of everything phony about you, that he can read you like a book. In such a situation, you cannot find a way of being genuine.

Think about it this way: if we arrange a kind of group psychotherapy session in which a little game is being played, and the gimmick in this game is that when anybody says or does anything, everyone else will challenge its sincerity, then anything you do will make you anxious and self-conscious.

Thinking about thinking, and being aware of being aware, is what is called in Japanese "the observing self." Watching yourself all the time, you become aware of your own hopelessness. The price that human beings pay for self-consciousness is anxiety and guilt. Anxiety asks, "When I left the house, did I turn off the stove? I remember turning it off, but can I trust my memory? Maybe I'd better go back and look." "All right, I just went back and looked, but did I really see? Did I look properly? You know how the unconscious can alter your senses. I better go and look again." You have trapped yourself in a vicious circle. You will never get away from the house. This risk of being trapped like this in a kind of feedback loop of consciousness is the penalty we pay for the gift of being able to know that we know.

The Zen trick is to put you into this situation in a very obvious way, to make you think about thinking about thinking about thinking. Or else—and this amounts to the same thing—to force you to make a very strong effort not to think. The latter of these techniques is zazen: sitting, letting your senses operate, being responsive to whatever may be around, but not thinking about it. Of course, this is still thinking. If I am thinking about not thinking, how will I stop thinking about not thinking? It is as though somebody came to you and put molasses in one of your hands and feathers in the other and slapped the two hands together, rubbed them around, then said, "Now pick off the feathers."

The Zen teacher is well aware that he has played a trick on you, and now he is going to see how you will respond to that trick, what foolishness you will come up with, and then he will help you act consistently on that foolishness. His trick has simply been to do, as if in an experiment, what society does to us all the time. The high cultures of the world, whether of the East or the West, play a game on every new child. They do not know they are playing this game, because their forefathers played it on them, and they are its victims. The game is called the double bind: you are required to do something that will be acceptable only if you do it voluntarily. You must love me; you must go to sleep; you must be natural; you must be free. Listen to that: you must be free.

The society into which a child is born defines that child. We learn who we are by the way other people react to us. When they tell us, "You are an independent agent; you are responsible; you are a freely acting individual," we take these statements to be commandments, and we seek to obey them because we cannot help it. A child has no way of criticizing this situation or of seeing. that there is something phony about it. Society defines the child as an independent agent and convinces him to believe in that, even though it is inaccurate. The child would not believe it if he were actually independent. The community has trouble getting children to behave as they want them to. Then they feel that there must be something innately or-nery about children. They must be born in a state of orig-inal sin. And of course they are—in effect—because they have been defined by society in a self-contradictory way.

It is self-contradictory when a community says to a person, "You must be free," or when members of a fam-ily say to each other, "You must love me; it's your duty." What a bunch of rot! If you say to your wife, "Darling, do you really love me?" and she replies, "I'm trying my very best to do so," that will not be the answer you wanted.

You wanted her to say, "Darling, I can't help loving you. I love you so much I could eat you." You do not want her to have to try to love you, and yet that is the burden you lay on people when you demand their love. In almost every marriage ceremony it is said that you must love your spouse. In Christianity it is said, "Thou shalt love the Lord, thy God," and "Thou shalt love thy neighbor as thyself." These are all double binds. Anybody who lives under the dominance of a double bind is living in a state of chronic frustration. He is devoting his life to solving a problem that is meaningless and nonsensical precisely because it has no solution.

The double bind that is the deepest of all is, You must go on living. Living is a spontaneous process, and an art, and to say to life, "You must happen," is exactly the same as saying to any creative artist, "You must come through with the goods; tonight you must give a superb performance and, furthermore, you must be completely un-self-conscious while you're doing it." This is being done to us all the time. The purpose of Zen is to make this double bind visible, so that you can see how stupid it is. The Zen teacher will be well aware of everything he is doing and what tricks he is playing on you, but he will play them anyway, because behind it all he has the compassionate intent of getting you into such a fierce double bind that you will see how stupid it is and let go of it. That is what he is doing when he commands, "Be genuine. Show me the real you."

A friend who was studying Zen was given a koan like this to work on, and as he was going for his interview, walking through the garden that connected the *sodo*, the monks' meditation hall and quarters, with the master's room, he saw a big bullfrog. Bullfrogs in Japan are rather tame; people do not eat them. He swept it up and dropped it into the sleeve of his kimono, and when he got in front of the teacher to answer the koan, to spontaneously produce his genuine self, he produced the bullfrog. The teacher looked at it, shook his head, and said, "No, too intellectual."

This is to say, "Your answer is too contrived, too studied—that is not you." Do you see the bind that's inherent in trying to be genuine? There is nothing you can do to be genuine. The more you do, the phonier you become. At the same time, you cannot give up trying to be genuine. The moment you do that, your abandonment of trying is itself an insidious form of trying.

There is a very interesting Hindu teacher by the name of Krishnamurti whom many of you may know about. He tells people that all of their religious inquiry, their yoga practices, their reading religious books, and so on, are nothing but the perpetuation of egocentricity on a very refined and highbrow level. Therefore he encourages disciples who studiously avoid reading any kind of philosophical or edifying book. They are reduced to reading mystery stories and they become devoted nondisciples. What a clever bind that is! It is the same as the Zen technique.

The way of Buddhism is to let go of yourself, to see that you live in a universe in which nothing can be grasped, and therefore to stop grasping. It is very simple, but here is the problem. You say to a teacher, "Teach me not to grasp." He will say, "Why do you want to know?" You will answer, "Non-attachment is good Buddhist doctrine." And he will show you that wanting to stop grasping is a new form of grasping. You feel that you can get one up on the world by being unattached to it. Just breathing is painful when somebody you love dies, so maybe by being unattached to that person I can avoid grief. Maybe when life comes and bangs on me, by not having an ego I can avoid life's pain. That is why I want a non-ego state. It is a phony desire, though, just a new way of safeguarding and protecting the ego. This is an example of the manner in which the statements of Buddhism are not final teachings but are rather the opening strategies of a dialogue.

Going back to fundamental, primitive Buddhism, people said to the Buddha, "I want to escape from suffering." That is a perfectly honest statement. All right, realize that suffering is caused by desire and try not to desire. The student goes away and tries to eliminate desire by controlling his mind and practicing yoga, and comes back to the teacher and says, "This is pretty difficult but I have managed to get rid of at least some desires." The teacher says to him, "But you are still desiring to get rid of desire. What about that?" Then the student sees that if he strives to stop desiring to get rid of desire, then he has got to stop desiring to get rid of not desiring to desire. Suddenly he finds himself once more in a vicious circle. He realizes there is nothing he can do about it and nothing he cannot do about it.

This predicament in Zen is called a mosquito trying to bite an iron bull, a situation of such psychic extremity that nothing can be done about it. What does this situation mean? When you find yourself in that kind of trap, what is the meaning of the trap? It is very simple. When there is nothing you can do about a given situation, and even doing nothing is doing something, that means that the ego, as something separate from the rest of the world, does not exist. Of course it cannot do anything, and equally it cannot not do something. It is completely phony. The fiction of there being a separate ego—either to force its actions on the world or to have the actions of the world forced on it—has been exposed.

The ego does not exist except as a figment of the imagination, or as a player in the game of pretending that everybody is responsible, independent, and separate. That is a great game, but it is only a game. The whole object of the Zen dialogue between the teacher and the student is to carry the foolish game of being a separate ego to its logical conclusion, to its *reductio ad absurdum*, so that, finally, as Blake said, "The fool who persists in his folly will become wise."

CHAPTER FIVE

Wisdom of the Mountains

This chapter concerns a subject somewhat alien to anything we understand in the West. Certain forms of Mahayana Buddhism—when seen from the outside—seem to us totally irrational and superstitious. This applies particularly to a subschool of Mahayana Buddhism that has several names: Vajrayana, Tantrayana, or Mantrayana.

The word *yana* means a way or a vehicle. As I mentioned earlier, Buddhism is frequently likened to a raft that is used for crossing a river, or a brick used to knock on a door. The brick is a yana, and so is the raft. They are instruments, expedients, means, techniques, methods. The Buddha's doctrine is called in Sanskrit the dharma, and dharma has a whole multiplicity of meanings, but one of them is "method." It is sometimes translated "law" in English, but this is not an adequate translation.

The whole idea of a yana is related to the idea of upayas, which are "skillful means." We would call them pedagogical devices or tricks, depending on the purpose for which they are being used. In politics *upaya* means cunning, but in religion or philosophy it means the skill of a teacher at conveying a lesson to a student. The essence of upaya is surprise. When you have hiccups, it is indeed surprising, because you did not intend it. Upaya and surprise are deeply connected with the whole inner meaning of Buddhism. Life has to surprise itself, because if it didn't you wouldn't know of your own existence. You only know existence to the degree that there is a balance between knowing and not knowing. So there must always be something in you that is like spiritual hiccups, that happens unbeknownst to you, and takes you by surprise.

An upaya is the teacher's method of arousing the surprise of enlightenment in the student, and he uses a yana, that is to say, a vehicle or a course. We say we give a course in philosophy or semantics or chemistry. The great course in Buddhism is the Mahayana, which includes ever so many different upayas or methods of instruction. By contrast, the Hinayana, the little course, has only a few upayas because they are very tough-minded in the Hinayana. They stick to the notion that all enlightenment depends on each individual's effort. The Buddha is supposed to have said, just before he died, "Be you lamps unto yourselves; be you a refuge unto yourselves. Take to yourselves no other refuge."

In one Japanese system of classification, Buddhist schools are called either *jiriki* or *tariki*. *Ji* means "self." *Riki* means "power." There are ways of salvation or liberation by your own power—jiriki—and ways by the power of another: tariki. Tariki is liberation through what Christians would call grace rather than works. It is fascinating to see how the problem of faith and works, or grace and works, turns up in Buddhism just as it does in Christianity.

In the history of Christianity there was a huge argument around 400 A.D. between a Welshman or Celt named Pelagius and Saint Augustine of Hippo. Pelagius was an optimistic Britisher, the type who believes in muddling through, playing the game, and putting your nose to the grindstone. He believed that one could, by one's own will and effort, obey the commandments of God. He argued that God would not have given us any commandments we could not obey. But Saint Augustine said that Pelagius had missed the point entirely. If he had read Saint Paul properly—especially the Epistle to the Romans—he would have found that God did not give us commandments in order that we should obey them, but rather to prove that we could not. As Saint Paul put it, God gave us impossible commandments in order to convict us of sin. The law, in other words, was a gimmick, an upaya. Nobody was ever expected to obey a law such as—from the Ten Commandments—"Thou shalt love the Lord thy God with all your heart, with all your soul, and with all your mind." Nobody can do that. Therefore even the greatest saints are always beating their breasts and confessing that they are abysmal sinners because they cannot live been tried and nothing will work. To achieve the perfection or completion of the art, something that cannot be willed has to happen of itself. We variously call this something grace or inspiration. It is tariki. Everybody always wants to know how to make it happen, but if we knew how to make it happen, it wouldn't be grace. It's because we don't know how to make it happen that it can transcend the limits of the will. Just because we can't know how to make it happen doesn't mean we should give up and go home and forget the whole thing, though. There is another alternative. We can cultivate our faith.

Faith means that we know grace will happen, only we don't know when, and we've got to wait. But we mustn't work too hard at waiting, because that will be ego effort, and the ego will stop the grace from happening. The thing is to learn to wait softly, in a state of openness. How does one do that? There are all sorts of upayas or means that help one to do this, and one of them is this practice variously called the *Vajrayana*, which means the diamond vehicle, the *Tantrayana*, which means the web vehicle, and the *Mantrayana*, which means the sound vehicle, in the sense of the vehicle of incantation.

The last of these—Mantrayana—is the most perplexing from our point of view. There is an age-old belief in the idea that certain formulas or spells, said in the right way, will produce results. All of this descends, philosophically—so far as Asia is concerned—from the Hindu Upanishadic idea that the world is the creation of sound. The Hindus say that in the beginning was *vac*, which is exactly the same thing as saying, "In the beginning was the word," as in the Gospel of John. But *vac* doesn't mean logos as it does in Saint John, it means vibration. It is fundamentally the Sanskrit word *om*. When you say om you begin at the back of your throat with O, and you finish at your lips, so you take in the whole range of world-creating sound. Om is the holiest of all names. You can chant om, you know, and really stir things up.

All Hindus and Buddhists alike use this word to induce a meditative state. It is very easy to concentrate on sound. It is much more difficult to keep your eyes still. But sound is very easy to concentrate on, and that is the whole point of a mantra: it is a method for digging sound. I hope you know what I mean by "to dig." It means to get right down into. When you dig sound you realize that the flow or vibration of sound is a way in which you experience basic existence, being here. You can learn everything from sound, because it is not a constant. It comes and goes. It is on and off. You only hear it because it is vibrating. The lesson is that life is on and off, black and white, life and death, inside and outside, knowing and not knowing: they're all vibrations. It's easy to explain that in words, but to feel and understand it in your bones you have to learn how to listen to a sound. It was to teach that skill that this system of chanting sounds was invented.

Vajrayana Buddhism sprang up in about the ninth century A.D. It spread from north India into Tibet, Mongolia, China, and Japan, but it is especially characteristic of Tibetan Buddhism.

There are various ways of understanding the words and formulas used for mantras. They are understood by the ignorant as being shortcuts. Instead of having to say a whole sutra, the sutra can be summed up in formulas such as "om mani padme hum." That's one way of understanding mantras. You are poor and ignorant, and out of infinite compassion the bodhisattvas have arranged to get you to nirvana. Instead of going through all the heroic efforts and meditation practices of those saints and sages, you can just say "om mani padme hum." In fact, you do not even need to say it. You can have it printed on paper and enclosed in a silver box on the end of a stick, and all you have to do is swing the thing around. So the popular idea of the vehicle of sound—the Mantrayana—is that it is a shortcut.

The next highest idea of Mantrayana is the one I have been emphasizing, that you use these formulas and sounds as concentration objects, and through that concentration learn the lessons of life. But there's also a third interpretation, which might be called the esoteric interpretation. I believe it was originated by Vasubandhu, who lived sometime around 400 A.D. He said the whole point of mantras is that they do not mean anything at all. The word *om* is completely meaningless, and all the various kinds of incantations are totally senseless. The purpose of repeating such nonsense is to liberate oneself from the notion that the universe means anything at all.

So much for the path to grace called the Mantrayana. We turn now to the Tantra.

All the forms of Buddhism that are associated with the Vajrayana are called Tantric. The word *Tantra* means "web structure," warp and woof. Tantra, in the Hindu context, is a discipline that is sometimes called the fifth

Veda. There are four Vedas that are basic holy scriptures of Hinduism. The fifth Veda is the esoteric one. According to the four Vedas, in order to be liberated you have to give up physical life. You must not eat meat. You must not have sexual intercourse. You must not take alcohol or any kind of consciousness-changing substance. There are various other things; I forget them all. But in Tantra the whole idea is that liberation comes through contact with forbidden things. It comes through belonging to the world, participating in it. Sometimes this is called the left-hand path.

In a Hindu story, Brahma was asked, "Who will gain to communion with you first, he who loves you or he who hates you?" And Brahma replied, "He who hates me, because he will think of me more often."

In other words, you can attain to liberation by complete altruism, and also by total selfishness. If you are completely and consistently selfish—if you push selfishness to an extreme—you will discover that your self is the other, that you do not really experience yourself at all except in terms of others. That is the point of the left-hand path, to push oneself to an extreme. However, the left-hand path is a very dangerous way of going about things, because nobody approves of it.

In my distant past my father and I once witnessed a stage comedy. A man was asleep in a highly Victorian bedroom filled with all kinds of fancy furniture. The alarm clock went off and he woke up in a total rage. He immediately picked up his shoe and smashed the alarm clock. He got out of bed in a fury. He ripped the sheets to pieces, overturned the bed, found a hammer somewhere and started breaking up all the crockery and the windows until the place was totally demolished, except that in one corner there remained one of those enormous stand-up lamps. It's the only unbroken thing in the room. The man becomes furious when he sees it just standing there innocently. He rushes across the room and picks it up over his head and flings it to the floor. And it bounces. It doesn't break. It was made of rubber.

That's the surprise I was talking about earlier. Satori. Sudden awakening. It bounced. This is the whole thing about Buddhism. We all think we are going to crash. We must think that, because otherwise it wouldn't be a surprise when we bounce.

In other words, if you press your selfishness, follow that left-hand path, explore all the sensations you can imagine—all the delights of pleasure, all the ecstasies, all the drunks, all the orgasms—what will you want, finally, after all that? You will say, "I want to bounce. I want to be let out of myself." When you are selfish and you are let out of yourself, that selfishness becomes altruism. "He that would save his life shall lose it. He that loses his life"—or loosens it—"shall find it." Whether we take the right-hand path or the other, we all arrive at the same destination.

In the same way, the painful path of meditative discipline or concentration—where the disciple is being watched over and threatened by somebody with a stick—will lead to the same goal. There are certain kinds of people who ought to take that path. They do not know they exist unless they hurt, and therefore the painful path is the right way for them. We should not condemn them or the path.

On the opposite extreme from the painful path is the mantra game. People who play this game say, "It's so simple to do. It's a shortcut." And they get into it, singing "om mani padme hum," for instance. Or, like the Pure Land Buddhists in Japan, they chant, "Namu Amida Butsu, Namu Amida Butsu, Namu Amida Butsu, Namu Amida Butsu, Namu Amida Butsu," until it eventually becomes, "Namanda, namanda, namanda, namanda, namanda," and suddenly the chant is chanting them. What is the difference between chant and chanter, self and other, self-power and other-power, jiriki and tariki? It is all one. You pretend that it isn't because you have to. I say "have to," but really you do it in order to create the sensation of existence.

Very vivid Tibetan paintings have a curious way of creating a state of mind, if you really start looking at them, that I can only call psychedelic. As you get into the detail, you will find there is nothing else quite like them. If you look closely at one, instead of its becoming fuzzy and fading out, it becomes clearer and more alive. You suddenly discover that what you thought was a blur was sixteen thousand maggots with bright eyes, and every eye a deep jewel. Go down into those jewels, and you will find inside them cross-legged buddhas with aureoles around them and necklaces of human heads. And when you start looking at those heads, by Jove, you see another buddha sitting there in every eye.

The state of consciousness these artists are trying to represent with their myriad details is the *dharma-dhatu*, the realm of dharma or reality, which is also described as Indra's net, which I discussed previously. Again, this is the net of jewels in which every jewel reflects all the other jewels, and therefore naturally contains the reflections of the reflections of all the other jewels, and so on, forever. This is an image of the interrelatedness, or "mutual penetration," of everything in the universe. Tibetan paintings are designed to get you into the mood to understand this interrelatedness. They are totally fascinating.

The possibility of seeing down into something goes on forever and ever. When you work with mantras, you can learn to hear similar infinite depths in sound. Just as you could say that a visual field is rich in detail like these paintings are—like a piece of beautiful Hindu silk weaving that is rich with gold and flowers that you see detail in—you can hear sound in the same way. That is what Hindu music is playing with, and when you get down into that, I would truly call it listening in to the universe. And if you listen to sound, or look at form that way, you discover its secrets.

This technique is another way of investigating life. It is comparable to our scientific investigation with microscopes and chemical analysis, and so on, which looks out into matter, and the physical world. The method of investigating sound and paintings goes in the opposite direction, into the nature of feeling, into the center of awareness, into the self. These Tibetan drawings are representations of the interior world from various points of view. They are drawings of our common interior world, looked at under the influence of the traditions of a culture that is not ours, which, therefore, strikes us as being a little strange. They are showing us a vision of the universe that we haven't seen before. Indeed we haven't, because the way we see is influenced and limited by the views of our culture. What you call ordinary is what you are used to. Therefore, by studying other people's art forms, we are taught to see things that we do not ordinarily notice. When you become used to Chinese or Tibetan painting, for instance, you will say, "Of course. That is also the way the world is."

A thing looks exotic when you look at it from somebody else's point of view, but eventually you get used to it. If you move into a state of consciousness such as I've been trying to describe, that is not your usual state of consciousness, you will say, "It's kind of weird." If you are not prepared for that you might become frightened and say, "Am I going mad? Am I going out of my mind?" Well, yes, you are. You are going out of your ordinary mind-set into another aspect of mind, and that always feels strange at first. That's why people have difficulty in meditation. When they start progressing they often say, "I'm going to go out of my mind." There are famous stories about people who thought about the nature of thought and were never heard from again. There is a certain fear of a loss of one's own ego, and of one's regular world, where familiar gestures make you feel at home. We all have in us levels of vibration that we are not familiar with, which we are therefore afraid of, and it is these levels we reach when we get out of our ordinary state of mind.

Vajrayana Buddhism is a rather adventurous, not to say dangerous, exploration of man's inner consciousness. The results of that exploration are depicted artistically in an elaborate system of symbols. To a Westerner accustomed to Christian symbolism, these symbolic representations of innerness will look like representations of heaven, with potentates on thrones receiving homage and all that sort of politics.

Let us suppose that we look through a microscope at the cross section of a spinal column, or at an area of the brain. We would see certain designs and patterns, and they would be based on the physical body. These patterns are equivalent to the symbols to be found in Tibetan paintings and drawings. But they are each moving in a different direction. One is based on the material or formal body, and the other is based on the subtle body.

The word *rupa* in Sanskrit means the formal body. It is applied to the material world, the world of form, the world seen in the way in which we are accustomed to seeing it. You have a formal body, which is how you appear to any other objective observer, and you have a subtle body, which is the way you feel you are to yourself. If you've been on a drinking spree and you wake up with a headache, and your head feels as big as a room, that is the shape of your subtle body at that moment.

There is a wonderful cartoon in which a comic-book character is watching a plane doing stunts, and his neck grows longer and longer as his head follows the plane, until his neck is tied in knots. That is an illustration of the shape of that character's subtle body.

So when you look through a microscope at a cross section of the spine, you will see a design that refers to the gross body. And when you look in the other direction and trace the senses back until you get to the *manovijnana*—the central sense behind each separate sense—you find that that process will produce an incredibly detailed experience. And then, if you drew pictures to represent what you had found, you would end up with a cross section or design of the subtle body. We in the West would draw pictures that were different from the pictures drawn by the Tibetans, if we genuinely made this inquiry ourselves, because we have different traditions. Goodness only knows what we would draw. Probably we would make things like the stained glass windows in Chartres Cathedral, and crucifixes, too, because if you investigate sensation and go down into it and feel it getting more and more intense—more, more, more, until you don't think you can endure any longer—that's Jesus on the cross. So cover it with jewels and make it gorgeous.

All these activities are investigations into the basic sensation of being alive. People are curious about the basic questions that come from being alive: Where are we; what's it all about? One of the only ways to answer these questions—to find out what you mean by meaning, by asking a question, by being conscious, by being here—is to meditate. However, meditation does not mean thinking out an answer in an intellectual way. It means to look more closely at the subject of your question. You could do that with a microscope, with chemical analysis, and so on. That way is valid. But it has to be balanced by the internal way of going down into one's own sensation, one's own consciousness. Now this is not something you are "supposed to do." It is not a chore or your solemn duty. It is simply delightful to look with total fascination and joy and love at whatever it is that you and everybody else are made of.

Yet this "looking" is a different spirit of religion from that to which we are normally accustomed. It is not a patriarchal attitude, which says, "Go read your Bible! Get down on your knees and repent." Instead, it says, "Psst. I've got something to show you. Look in here. Watch. Take a look." This is the attitude, and I don't know how to suggest it except by contrasting the two different approaches.

This is as near as I can get to describing the inner meaning of Tantra. It is an attitude that is common to both Hinduism and Buddhism. It means the web, the warp and woof, the yes and the no. It is the comprehension of the unity of opposites, of good and bad, of life and death, of love and hate, of all extremes in the whole spectrum of our emotions and our sensations.

This is not a teaching for children. You must have some maturity to understand this lesson. A child hearing this teaching would cease paying respect to rules or constraints because a child would see only that anything goes. There is no way of doing wrong if you are everything there is, forever and ever. You can die, forget everything altogether; what would it matter? There is always light on the other side of the darkness. You can always begin anew. This would be a child's reaction to this teaching. But the adult would understand that even after everything was new again, the same patterns would unfold. Everything would be once again exactly as it was before, just as the physical forces in things repeat their fundamental laws and patterns. As it is in the outer world, so it is in the inner.

Buddhist enlightenment consists simply in knowing the secret of the unity of opposites—the unity of the inner and outer worlds—and in understanding that secret as an adult rather than as a child. It means, really, to finally grow up. To misunderstand this teaching is to fall into a trap. Just as in our own culture there is an attitude among many of our religious people of being against life, there is in Buddhism the trap of following the teachings without understanding them. As Saraha, a Tantric teacher who lived about 1000 A.D., said in critique of both the Hindu and Buddhist orthodoxy, "The Brahmans who do not know the truth recite the four Vedas in vain. With earth and water and *kusha* grass they make preparations. Seated at home they kindle fire. From the senseless offerings they make they burn their eyes with the pungent smoke. In lordly garb, with one staff or three, they think themselves wise with their Brahmanical law. Vainly is the world enslaved by their vanity. They do not know that the dharma is the same as the non-dharma. With ashes these masters smear their bodies. On their heads they wear matted hair. Seated within the house they kindle lamps. Seated in the corner they tinkle bells. They adopt a posture and fix their eyes, whispering in ears and deceiving folk, teaching widows and bald-headed nuns, and taking their fees.

"The Jain monks mock the way with their appearance, with their long nails and their filthy clothes. Or else naked and with disheveled hair they enslave themselves with their doctrine of liberation. If by nakedness one is released, then dogs and jackals must be so. If from absence of hair there comes perfection, then the hips of maidens must be so. If from having a tail there comes release, then for the peacock and yak it must be so. If wisdom consists in eating just what one finds, then for elephants and horses it must be so. For these Jain monks there is no release. Deprived of the truth of happiness, they do but afflict their own bodies."

Saraha continues, "Then there are the novices and bhikshus"—meaning Buddhist monks—"following the teachings of the old school of Theravada Buddhism, renouncing the world to be monks. Some can be seen reading the scriptures. Some are withering away while concentrating on thought. Others have recourse to the Mahayana, the doctrine which expounds the original text, they say. Others just meditate on mandala circles. Others strive to define the fourth stage of bliss. With such investigating they fall from the way. Some would envisage it as space, others endow it with the nature of voidness, and thus they are generally in disagreement. But whoever seeks nirvana while deprived of the innate by attachment to any of these vehicles, these methods, can in no way acquire the absolute truth. Whoever is intent on method, how may he gain release? Will one gain release abiding in meditation? What is the use of lamps or offerings? What is to be done by reliance on mantras? What is the use of austerities or of going on pilgrimages? Is release achieved by bathing in water? No. Abandon such false attachments and renounce such illusions:"

And that is the wisdom of the mountains.

Transcending Duality

I want to begin this subject with a discussion of male-female symbolism in Tantric yoga, and then move on to other aspects of the Mahayana.

You will find that in the Tantric art forms, every buddha or aspect of buddha has a feminine counterpart. Not only do they have feminine counterparts, but they also have different forms depending on the level at which they are being manifested. For instance, there are the five dhyani buddhas, who represent the blossom of a rose; one in the middle and the remaining four surrounding it. Each has a corresponding bodhisattva form, and each bodhisattva has, in turn, a corresponding *heruka* form, which is a rough, weird, and kind of far-out character, often depicted as having a bull's head. But all of these are forms of the original five buddhas. Whether they are in the form of a bodhisattva or a heruka, they are all reducible to the original group of dhyani buddhas.

Now, all of these figures have female counterparts, and these male/female pairs are always represented as touching at all points, in the complete embrace of sexual intercourse. It is understood that this embrace will last forever and ever, and will never end, and that this idea or image is a way of representing the resonant nature of life. The fundamental point of Tantric yoga is self-knowledge. Without resonance nothing happens. Suppose we had a room in which all the walls, and the floor, and the ceiling were soundproofed. You would hardly be able to hear anyone talk, because the voice benefits from resonance. Resonance is why people enjoy singing in the bathtub. It resonates with their voice, and they suddenly discover that they have a good voice. That is why violins, cellos, or bass fiddles have hollow wooden bodies: to make their sounds resonate, to play them back to themselves.

Perhaps this is the reason we are all so fascinated with taking photographs, writing things down, and, above all, remembering. These are all forms of resonance. A person who had total amnesia, who did not remember anything, would not be capable of self-knowledge. And perhaps there are some forms of life that do not know they are there. I do not know whether the particular cells constituting my body know that they exist. Maybe they do. Maybe they have some wonderful system of resonance that I know nothing about and they are all worried about what I am going to do with them, and are having conferences and meetings and making policy decisions and so on about this person in charge. It might well be that when we die our cells suddenly say, "God is dead." They have a theological controversy and say, "We will just have to fend for ourselves from now on." It may be that we have some kind of system like that, but certainly to know that, I don't know. In any case, to know you exist you need an echo.

So I invented the following limerick:

> *There was a young man who said, "Though*
> *It seems that I know that I know.*
> *What I would like to see*
> *Is the I that knows me*
> *When I know that I know that I know."*

We are absolutely fascinated with the whole idea of remembering and recording. When there is a gathering of people, they say, "This is great. It's a pity somebody didn't bring a camera." But in recording a thing there is both a gain and a loss. That's why some people say things should be photographed, while others prefer to look at them and then let them go. I had some experience of this phenomenon while touring in Japan. My students brought cameras and were constantly photographing things, and I had a camera as well and was also constantly photographing, but at the same time I felt that so long as I had a camera with me I would be distracted from actuality by it. I had a little box with which I went around grabbing life. Of course, it was great to come back and look at the photographs, but there is something about a photograph that is inferior to the actual experience that is being photographed. There is something immensely fascinating about photography and painting. They are forms of reproduction, which is also true of sexuality. They are like sexual reproduction in that they say you are here, you are alive, and they resonate with life. One school of religion says, "Let it all go. Don't be attached. Live in the moment." Krishnamurti used to say, "Stop trying to remember everything."

You may need a kind of factual memory for your name and address and telephone number and things like that, but do not linger over memories, treasuring them, thinking, "I'm going to keep my girlfriend's lock of hair and take it out every now and then and look at it and it will make me feel wonderful." That is a clinging to memory, which holds you to the past and to death.

The other school of thought, quite opposite to this, goes along with the title of one of Henry Miller's books, *Remember to Remember*. This school says, "Hold on to it all. Get involved. Keep your girlfriend's hair; keep all the photographs." You know how in some houses the piano is completely covered with photographs and reminiscences. I went to visit Gloria Swanson once, and had never before seen such a house full of memories. Everything in all directions was of Gloria Swanson, photographed on this occasion, signed on that occasion, and receiving various presentations. I also once went to visit the wife of a former archbishop of Canterbury, and the whole house was memorials, a complete clutter of tombstone furniture with little brass plates on it, "Presented on the occasion" of this, that, and the other. Now, you might say, "That person isn't really living. They are stuck in the past." But on the other hand, what is life without memory, resonance, echo?

I scarcely need to point out the duality of all this. If you are a wise man you do not take sides in this issue, you occupy both sides. That is the meaning of the unity of samsara and nirvana. On the one hand, you let go of everything and live in the eternal now because that is all there is. Memory is an illusion; it is all gone. Everything that has made an impression on you is gone. That is the meaning of *maya*, or illusion. There is only the eternal now, the present moment, and there never will be anything else. All remembering occurs in the present; memory exists in the eternal now.

On the other hand, what fun to drag life out and make it echo and get involved with it, and to fall in love and become attached.

R. H. Blyth once wrote me a letter in which he said, "What are you doing these days? As for me, I am abandoning all kinds of satori and enlightenment and am trying to become as deeply attached to as many people and as many things as possible."

It is a balancing trick, like riding a bicycle. You find yourself falling over one way and you turn in that direction and stay up. In the same way, when you find yourself becoming too attached to life, you correct that excessive attachment with the realization that nothing exists except the eternal now. And then, when you feel you are safe again, because the eternal now is the only thing that exists, you go off and get involved with some kind of social, political, amorous, familial, scholarly, or artistic enterprise. The two always go together.

This is the meaning of the sexual symbolism in Tantric yoga. The male knows he exists only if there is a female, an echo. And the female knows of her existence only when there is a male. Nobody ever came into existence without parents. There is simply no other way into this universe.

I want to illustrate this idea of simultaneous attachment and detachment, involution and evolution. Involution is how you get involved; evolution is how you get out. Tantric yoga represents all of this in the most extraordinary symbolism based not only on the sexual functioning of the human body but also on the whole nervous system as well. In yoga philosophy there is the idea of the psychic anatomy, and this psychic anatomy belongs to the subtle body. Do not expect to find this subtle body in the physical organism. It is not an addition to the physical organism or a kind of ghost that goes around with it. The physical body is the body as seen by others. The subtle body is the way you feel yourself to be.

The anatomy of the subtle body consists of the processes of involution and evolution. These processes are visualized as a spinal tree with two paths crossing back and forth in front of it. The familiar image of two serpents on a rod, the caduceus carried by Mercury, is another representation of this same idea. Alchemically, mercury—the mirror substance—is the void, the pure clear light. It is the same thing as the Buddhist diamond. The tree or canal of the subtle body is called the *sushuna*. One of the two routes crossing in front of it is called the *ida*. The other is the *pingala*. In one channel something is going down, and on the other something is coming up. At the base of the spinal column, according to the chakra system of Tantric yoga, sits the *kundalini*, the serpent power. The symbol of the serpent power is an inverted triangle with a phallus, upright and erect, with a sleeping serpent coiled all the way around it. That is involution: to be absolutely involved. The sex symbol is used because, symbolically, sex stands for complete involvement.

Once you have experienced complete involvement, the trick is to get out. The process of yoga is represented as awakening the serpent that is sleeping the sleep of maya. Captivated by illusion, it thinks that the world really exists. To put it another way, the male has been captivated by the female echo of himself, and the female has been captivated by the male echo of herself. To say it a third way, you have been caught by memory; you think the objects of memory are all really here. You do not realize that there is only an eternal now. In other words, you are involved. You have become one-sided in the direction of involvement. Now, if you go out to any one end of the spectrum, you will forget you are there. You will enter a kind of nonexistence. You cannot really nonexist because you will always come back eventually, but if you go too far to one extreme, you will not know you are here. Therefore you must evolve. The process of evolving is symbolized by the idea that you can draw the involved energy located in the kundalini, which is the sex center, and send it back up the spinal tree to the top, from whence it came.

The practice of sexual yoga employs a male and a female partner who are husband and wife or are in some kind of spiritual marriage. The male sits in the normal meditation posture. The female sits on top of him, wrapping her legs around his waist and her arms around his neck. He holds her around her waist. In this position they arouse the sexual force. The theory is that instead of dissipating this energy in the ordinary way—through orgasm—they send it up the spinal tree, back into the brain. Do not take this literally. It is symbolism. To take this symbolism literally would be to turn it into a superstition. It would be exactly the kind of superstition that comes from thinking that heaven is somewhere up in the sky and there really are streets of gold and angels wandering around in nighties, playing harps. All of these images are ways of talking about our inner anatomy, our psychic anatomy. The kingdom of heaven is within you. When Jesus ascended into heaven, he went right into the middle of himself and disappeared.

The image of the pearly gates of heaven makes people think that the gates of heaven are literally gates covered with pearls. In fact, the image means nothing of the kind. It is actually meant to convey the idea that the gates of heaven are like pearls, with all the connotations associated with a pearl's spherical shape and luster. It is because of these same connotations that, in Hinduism, the idea of many incarnations is likened to beads strung together on a thread. The thread is called the *sutra atman*. *Sutra* is "thread"; *atman* is "self." The sutra atman is the thread of self on which all the beads of reincarnation hang. The self is so thin, though, that it is like no-self. Which brings us back to the idea of raising the kundalini—the snake, or serpent power—up the tree. To raise the serpent you have to let go of the hang-ups of involvement and realize that there are no possessions, everything is falling away, and all memories are just a holding-on-to of illusions. When you evolve to the point of thoroughly understanding that, then you can become involved again.

In this Tantric symbolism you have a marvelous picture of the world alternating between systole and diastole, attachment and detachment. This takes us right back to the idea of the bodhisattva who is liberated, who has let go and is no longer attached, and has given up memory. The meaning behind the idea of giving up the man or woman who is your resonator is that, when you give them up, you will find that you are free: there is only the eternal now.

Of course, the bodhisattva, instead of staying detached, goes back into the world. There are all sorts of funny symbolic stories about bodhisattvas appearing in the world as beggars and whores, using every conceivable kind of device in order to liberate other beings.

This idea of systole/diastole, attachment/detachment, takes us all the way back to the original Hindu image of the world as the *pralaya* and the *manavantara*. The manavantara is the period in which Brahma manifests himself as multiple beings for 4,320,000 years. The pralaya is the period in which he withdraws and everything disappears. This alternation between pralaya and manavantara goes on forever and ever, and not only in our universe, but also in many other dimensions of space and time. The Buddhist idea of giving up attachment to the world and yet remaining in it is the same idea of the manavantara/pralaya alternation re-created in another form.

You may feel that this cycle is pretty monotonous, and, in fact, monotony is one of the basic feelings underlying Buddhism. "Must we go around again? Enough of this. Let's go to sleep. Time must have a stop." But when you stop you forget that it all ever happened, and this forgetfulness is marvelous, because then the world can start over again without your knowing that it has all happened before, and you are never bored. This is the cure for being tired of things. There are going to be all sorts of problems, but you won't know you've had any problems before, so having problems again will not bore you until you accumulate memories once more. When you have had enough of these problems that it becomes a bore dealing with them, you get rid of yourself again. It is called death, a beautiful arrangement for keeping everything young and new and for keeping the universe running without getting tired of itself.

These are the two fundamental notions of being, and they are represented by the dualities of male and female, light and dark, now and memory. Memory, remember, creates the future as well as the past. You would not know you were going to have anything happen tomorrow unless you remembered that something had happened yesterday. You figure that because the sun rose yesterday, and the day before yesterday, it will rise again tomorrow. If you did not remember the past, you would not know that there will be a tomorrow. Because there is no tomorrow. Tomorrow is an illusion produced by memory, and so is yesterday.

They simply do not exist. Where is tomorrow? Bring me tomorrow's newspaper.

You may feel, as you think these things over, that you are almost on the verge of going mad. I sometimes feel that way when I get involved in a contemplative state. The thing to do is not to worry. Let go and swing with it, because you will always bounce back. What gives you the sense of impending madness is that you think you are not in control and that someone or something else has taken over. Well, of course something has to take over. When you have driven long enough in the car, you say to your wife, "Will you drive for a while, please?" You want the relief that comes when something else takes over for you. But that "something else" is always secretly you, and you need not fear it. The nature of being is constructed in this extraordinarily fascinating way. It constantly renews itself by eternally forgetting itself. This is a perfectly marvelous arrangement. It is a funny thing how we all alternate in this way between remembering and not remembering. We remember things long enough to know that we are here. We would not know it if we didn't remember. But when memory weighs on us too much and we are too much here, we seek liberation in the realization that all memory is an illusion, there is no future and equally no past, there is nothing except the present moment. But when you are liberated, you like to come back and play the memory game again. Liberation is a cleaning process. You wipe off the blackboard and start writing again, then you wipe it off, and then you start writing again. This is the process whereby life keeps going.

I have been listening to recorded sutra chanting from Koya-san, Mount Koya, which is the ultimate center and inner sanctuary of the Japanese practice of the Vajrayana branch of Mahayana Buddhism. The monks who were chanting are a bunch of boys just like American college boys who play football, and some of them do not have the faintest idea what they are doing. Some of them are there only because their fathers have sent them there. Perhaps their fathers own temples and they have to carry on their fathers' tradition, because the family business must go on, and so some of them have no idea what this chanting is all about. You and I could get into the swing of it, dance to it, go very far out on it, as it was originally intended for us to do. But for many of the monks of Mount Koya, these chants are just a chore, a thing they have to get up at five o'clock in the morning to do. They have to memorize all this, get it exactly right, and they do, but they have completely forgotten why they do it and the substance underlying it.

The monks on Mount Koya have come to a point in the historical development of their way of life where they often remember so much about it that nothing in their way of life is any longer new to them. They are just going through the motions. This is a version of the same paradox I mentioned earlier, that the echo of memory that tells you that you exist also entraps you. To the extent that it tells you that you do exist, it is an advantage. To the extent that it traps you, it is the price you must pay for your existence, and you should be thankful. Somebody gave it to you.

In the Judeo-Christian tradition, the Lord God gave it

to you, and you are supposed to be thankful and say, "Anything bad that I did was from me. Dear God, anything good that I did was from you." What a marvelous mix-up that is, and there must come a point in all this where you have to say to people, "Please come off it."

I was aching to know enough Japanese to say to those boys on Mount Koya, "Realize what a great thing you have here! Enjoy it! Get together and join hands and chant these sutras and really make something happen."

Now, in talking about alternating between memory and forgetfulness I have been talking about the process I call flip-flop-ability, whereby we switch from one attitude to another, one situation to another. This pulse or switching is the very nature of existence, the beat of your heart, the vibration of sounds and light. Everything goes back and forth so that you can know you are here. This game of knowing has its own inner meaning. To complete my discussion of it I want to talk about one form of the Mahayana that I have not discussed at all. This is the Pure Land school, which is the most popular form of Mahayana Buddhism in the Far East. Everywhere in China and Japan the multitudes follow this branch, which venerates as its presiding image Amitabha, one of the dhyani buddhas, whose name means "boundless light." He is an aspect of Mahavairochana, the great sun Buddha, who was probably derived, historically, from Ahura Mazda from Persia, the great sun god of the Mazdians and the Parsees. But although Ahura Mazda may have been the origin of the sun Buddha, the idea of the Persian sun god has been greatly transformed by Buddhism.

You have all probably seen photographs of the Daibutsu, the Great Buddha, at Kamakura, Japan. It is an enormous bronze figure that sits in a beautiful park surrounded by pine trees. The original temple around it was long ago demolished by a tidal wave, for which thanks be to God. If it hadn't been for that tidal wave, nobody would have ever really seen this figure. This huge bronze Buddha is about forty-two feet high. It sits surrounded by great activity. School children by the thousands are always streaming by on tours; photographers are always taking pictures; people are constantly selling various souvenirs; exhibitions of dwarf trees are going on all around, and amid all this, there Buddha sits, looking down forever. He hushes everything. No matter how much turmoil there is in the park, the huge face of this Buddha presides over everything, and you cannot ignore it. He subdues you into peace, but not in an authoritative way. He does not say, "Shut up!" but is just so peaceful that you cannot help but catch the infusion of peace that flows from him. This is the Buddha Amida, or Amitabha. He is not the historical Shakyamuni Gautama Buddha, who lived in India, but is one of the dhyani buddhas who are not manifested in the world.

The religion connected with this figure is called the Pure Land school; in Japanese it is *Jodo-shin-shu*, the True Sect of the Pure Land. This religion has its origins, as always, in India, but under the genius of Honen and Shinran, who were medieval Buddhist saints, the Japanese developed their own special variety of it.

It is a very strange religion. It takes as its basis the idea that we are now living in the most decadent period of history. This claim comes from the Hindu idea that this is the *Kali yuga*, the end of time, when everything is completely fouled up. This period started on February 23, 3023 B.C. It will last for five thousand years more, at which point everything will fall apart and the universe will disappear out of sheer failure. In this decadent period nobody can be truly virtuous. People who try to be virtuous at this time are merely showing off, are not really pure, are just pretending to be virtuous. They give money to charity not because they love the people they are giving the money to but because they feel they ought to do it. Their motivations are inescapably bad, and because of that, nobody can possibly liberate themselves from the chains of karma. The more they try to get out of their karma, their conditioning, their bondage to their past, the more they get themselves involved in it. Therefore all human beings living now—in the Kali yuga, the end time, which the Japanese call *mappo*—are just hopelessly selfish.

In this predicament you cannot rely on jiriki, your own power, to achieve liberation from self. You have to rely on the power of tariki, which is the power of something other than you. In the Jodo-shin-shu sect, the tariki, the other power, is represented in the form of Amitabha—in Japanese, Amida—this great beneficent Buddha figure in the park at Kamakura whom everybody loves. He is quite strangely different from any kind of authoritarian god figure we have in the West. He sits there serenely quiet. He does not preach. All you have to do is say his name in homage—"Namu Amida Butsu," which means "the name of Amida Buddha"—and after death you will be reborn in a special paradise called *Sukhavati*, which is *jodo*, the pure land, where becoming enlightened is easy. It has none of the difficulties surrounding it that we have in our ordinary life today.

Everybody born in the pure land is born inside a lotus. There is a huge lotus pond there. Amida sits in front of it with all his attendants, and the lotuses come up out of the pond and go *pop* as a bud breaks open, and inside every bud is a new little being, somebody who has said the Namu Amida Butsu formula on earth and is now sitting on a lotus like a buddha. In the museum at Mount Koya there is a great painting depicting what it is like to arrive in this pure land. It shows a huge panorama of Amitabha and all his attendants—such as the *apsaras*, who look at you with lovely, longing eyes—and all you have to do to get there is say "Namu Amida Butsu." Just say it. You don't even have to believe that it will work.

That is the religion of most Japanese Buddhists, believe it or not. If you really feel that you will go to Sukhavati for having said "Namu Amida Butsu," then you will be grateful and try to help other people while you are here, and be a bodhisattva. The whole point, though, is that you cannot do this by your own effort, and the moment you think you can, you become a phony. You must go completely the other way. You must acknowledge that you have no power or capability of being virtuous or unselfish.

This kind of religion developed a peculiar kind of saint they call the *myoko-nin*: *myo* meaning "wonderful"; *ko* meaning "fine"; nin meaning "person." Myoko-nin are very special characters.

Among stories told about them is one of a traveling man who came to a temple during the course of a night. He walked in, took the sacred cushions on which the priests sit, arranged them in front of the altar, and went to sleep. In the morning the priest came in and said, "What's going on here?" The myoko-nin looked at him and answered, "You must be a stranger here. You don't belong to the family."

The myoko-nin knew that the great thing in life comes not from one's own doing but from the side of experience that we think belongs to the other. There are some who believe that it comes from the split in experience that you call yourself. Those are the jiriki people. The tariki people believe it comes from the other.

When you penetrate deeply into the doctrines of the Pure Land school you will see that only the simple people believe that Amitabha Buddha is really sitting on a golden lotus surrounded by all those apsaras and so on. The simple priests in the country villages still insist that that is what one should believe, but the sophisticated priests do not believe that at all. They know that Amitabha is in you. It is that side of you that you do not define as being part of you.

It is in the nature of duality that self and other go together. You do not need to cling to yourself and oppose the other. Everything you call the other is you too. You will realize this if you take any aspect of duality to an extreme. You can, for instance, pursue the idea of total courage, of letting go of everything, of being a true Zen monk, abandoning all property, living in a barn, sitting up in the middle of the night, in the cold, eating rice and pickles, and so on. You can seek liberation in that manner, by going to that extreme. But if you do, you will eventually arrive at the same place as the person who pursued liberation by going to the other extreme, of making no effort whatsoever.

Liberation comes of itself. The person who seeks to make no effort will encounter as many difficulties as the person who seeks to pursue the path of total courage, because how can one make no effort? How does one get to the point of doing no work at all, of just doing nothing, however? Even if all you do is say "Namu Amida Butsu," you are still doing work. It is easy to do, but it's still work. To really do nothing, with perfection, is as difficult as doing everything.

"Books to Span the East and West"

Tuttle Publishing was founded in 1832 in the small New England town of Rutland, Vermont [USA]. Our core values remain as strong today as they were then—to publish best-in-class books which bring people together one page at a time. In 1948, we established a publishing outpost in Japan—and Tuttle is now a leader in publishing English-language books about the arts, languages and cultures of Asia. The world has become a much smaller place today and Asia's economic and cultural influence has grown. Yet the need for meaningful dialogue and information about this diverse region has never been greater. Over the past seven decades, Tuttle has published thousands of books on subjects ranging from martial arts and paper crafts to language learning and literature—and our talented authors, illustrators, designers and photographers have won many prestigious awards. We welcome you to explore the wealth of information available on Asia at www.tuttlepublishing.com.

Published by Tuttle Publishing, an imprint of Periplus Editions (HK) Ltd.

www.tuttlepublishing.com

Copyright © Mark Watts 1996

Library of Congress Cataloging-in-Publication Data

Watts, Alan, 1915–1973.
    Buddhism, the religion of no-religion: the edited transcripts/by Alan Watts. —1st ed.
      xii, 98 p. ; 23 cm.—(Love of wisdom library)
    ISBN 0-8048-3056-8
    1. Buddhism. I. Title. II. Series:
    Watts, Alan, 1915-1973.
Alan Watts "Love of wisdom" library.
BQ4055.W356 1996
294.3—dc20
          95051266
            CIP

Photo courtesy of Alan Watts Electronic Educational Programs

ISBN 978-0-8048-5608-9

Distributed by:

North America, Latin America & Europe
Tuttle Publishing
364 Innovation Drive
North Clarendon, VT 05759-9436
U.S.A.
Tel: 1 (802) 773-8930
Fax: 1 (802) 773-6993
info@tuttlepublishing.com
www.tuttlepublishing.com

Asia Pacific
Berkeley Books Pte. Ltd.
3 Kallang Sector #04-01
Singapore 349278
Tel: (65) 6741-2178
Fax: (65) 6741-2179
inquiries@periplus.com.sg
www.tuttlepublishing.com

26 25 24 23   4 3 2 1   2401TO
Printed in Malaysia

Tuttle Publishing® is a registered trademark of Tuttle Publishing, a division of Periplus Editions (HK) Ltd.